The Executive's Guide to Finding a Superior Job

Revised Edition

William A. Cohen

American Management Associations

Other books by William A. Cohen
  Principles of Technical Management (AMACOM, 1980)
  How to Sell to the Government (John Wiley & Sons, Inc., 1981)
  Successful Marketing for Small Business (with Marshall Reddick, AMACOM, 1981)
  Building a Mail Order Business (John Wiley & Sons, Inc., 1982)

This book is available at a special discount when ordered in bulk quantities. For information, contact AMACOM, Special Sales Department, 135 West 50th Street, New York, NY 10020.

Library of Congress Cataloging in Publication Data

Cohen, William A., 1937–
  The executive's guide to finding a superior job.

  Includes index.
  1. Job hunting. 2. Executives—Recruiting. I. Title.
HF5382.7.C63   1983   650.1'4'024658   83-3695
ISBN 0-8144-5766-5

© 1978, 1983 AMACOM Book Division
American Management Associations, New York.
All rights reserved.
Printed in the United States of America.

First Printing

Preface to the Revised Edition

Naturally, authors are always delighted when their publishers ask them to revise a book for a new edition. Not only does this mean that the book is a commercial success, but it also means that the audience for whom the book was written has been generally well served by what the author had to say. Perhaps because managers and executives are in general an appreciative group eager to share their experiences with others in the same boat, I already knew that the book had been well received before my publisher contacted me. Executives all over the country from every industry, from government, and from the nonprofit sector had written or telephoned (or both) to express their appreciation. In some cases they offered additional or modified techniques that had worked for them.

Much has happened in my own life since the first edition was published in 1978. Although still president of my own firm, which does management and marketing consulting, I became a professor of marketing, as well as director of the Bureau of Business and Economic Research, at California State University Los Angeles in 1979. This work has exposed me to many new ideas and theoretical approaches to job finding, a few of which have been modified for executives, found effective, and included in this edition.

You may wonder whether I used the techniques I recommend here when I attained my position in academia. I did, despite the advice of well-meaning friends—already professors—who said that a particular form of resume known as the curriculum vitae was an absolute requirement. I disregarded this advice. At a time when few professors were being hired (and certainly even fewer "old men" in their forties with no academic teaching experience), I had three universities competing for my services even though I limited my campaign to the Southern California area.

The basic system of job finding remains unchanged in this revised edition of *The Executive's Guide to Finding a Superior Job*. As with the first edition, it is my firm belief that this book will enable you to maximize your potential to get the best job that you are capable of handling—your superior job—immediately. However, almost every chapter in the book has been updated with new techniques and concepts. Chapter 8, "How to Advertise Yourself," has been extensively revised to include six powerful techniques to assist in self-promotion and -advertisement. In addition, four major new chapters have been added to the book. Chapter 13, "The Concentration Strategy," describes a unique application of the methods outlined in the first edition. The executive who used this strategy became vice president of a division of a major motion picture studio, even though he was out of work and had never been vice president of any firm previously. Chapter 14, "Strategies for a Tough Job Market," shows additional methods of beating the competition when the market argues against even competing for a superior job. Chapter 21 describes executive job counseling services. Despite the advice given in many articles and books I have seen, I believe that there are circumstances when such services may be useful. This chapter lists these situations and suggests some safeguards should you decide to use these services. Chapter 22 outlines some successful campaigns that have been conducted using the first edition of *The Executive's Guide to Finding a Superior Job*.

Some readers will notice that, except for a few specific examples, most of the job seekers and prospective employers referred to in this book are men. This is not meant to exclude women from the ranks of job-seeking or hiring executives. Merely for the sake of grammatical simplicity, "he" has been used rather than "he or she." The important thing to remember is that the techniques described here work for *anyone*.

In concluding this brief preface, I want to note that I believe it possible for anyone to attain a superior job. Certainly managers and executives, upon whom so much depends, should position themselves so that their work is useful and fulfilling. In this way, not only the productivity of the individual but also the productivity of our society will be maximized.

William A. Cohen
Pasadena, California
August 1982

Preface to the
First Edition

The first time I looked for a job, I didn't know where to begin. I had been out of school for 11 years, and I had spent those years not in industry, but in the Air Force. Many friends who were not searching for new jobs told me it would be easy. But observation told me otherwise. I saw many extremely well-qualified people forced to take much lower positions than they deserved; a few other individuals always seemed to do well and consistently found superior jobs. It took *me* several years to discover that, regardless of a person's qualifications, certain techniques are essential for successful job hunting. These techniques, which are revealed in this book, can make a major difference in the level and quality of the job offered and the compensation received.

Since my first experience in job hunting, I have read many books on executive job seeking. Several were worth reading; others gave advice that could lead only to disaster. All had one major shortcoming: although the authors claimed years of experience related to executive job placement, none had recent job-finding experience of their own.

My qualifications for writing this book are unique. I am both a practicing manager and a former executive recruiter. I have held positions as an engineering and marketing executive in companies large and small, foreign and domestic. As a result, I know the secrets of the professional headhunter but have no vested interest and no reason not to reveal to you every secret that I know. Let me give you an example. No other book on the market tells you the technique that professionals use to break a "blind" advertisement. The reason is simple. If everybody uses it, it won't work. Yet this technique can be crucial to the job hunter who must conduct a campaign in secret.

The fact that I am a practicing manager—not an employment counselor, personnel manager, executive recruiter, or college placement director—also means that I see things from *your* viewpoint, not someone else's.
For example, I once read a book on job hunting, written by a personnel
manager, that recommended techniques that would have hurt your
chances of finding a superior job. Why should this be so? Personnel
managers play a unique role in the hiring situation. Except in their own
specialty, they cannot hire you, only prevent you from being hired. One of
their main functions in hiring is to screen out candidates they feel are
unsuited for a particular job. Most personnel managers assume that they
know best whether your background will allow you to perform a job
adequately. So it is not surprising that a job-hunting book written by a
personnel manager would recommend that you give information on your
background that is not in your best interest to give. To be quite blunt, in
many job-hunting situations it is to your advantage to sidestep personnel
managers or to manipulate them to your own advantage.

In another book, the president of an employment agency recommended that you state your minimum salary right in your resume. What's
wrong with this? If your minimum is too high, you will probably be
eliminated without an inteview. Yet if you could get to the interview you
might persuade an employer to pay more for your valuable services. If
your stated minimum is well below the range for the job, you may also be
eliminated. Many employers assume that you are not "heavy" enough for
the job if the salary you want is too modest. Further, even if you get an
interview and a job offer, your negotiating position is limited.

Why would an employment agency recommend doing this? Employment agencies get paid by the hiring companies only if they hire. Therefore
they generally prefer to work with candidates who are relatively easy to
place. One consideration, of course, is the willingness to accept a salary
that is not too high for a particular job or industry. Further, an employment
agency that is working a "fee paid" job order is working primarily for the
company, not for you. So it is in the agency's interest to know the
minimum amount you will accept. If this figure is known, the company
certainly isn't going to offer you a lot more.

The techniques I will teach you in this book will help you to get a
superior job whether you are currently employed or have just resigned,
been fired, or been laid off; whether you are young or old, handicapped,
male or female, white, black, brown, red, yellow, or blue; or whether you
are currently in industry, academia, government, or the military. I will
introduce you to executives who have made these techniques pay off and
show you how they did it. I am not instructing you in these techniques
second-hand or through someone else's placement. On several occasions I

have chosen to resign my former position before searching for a new one. Yet I have never taken on a new job without a substantial salary increase. As a matter of fact, I have increased my own salary by 67 percent over the last four years by using the techniques I will teach you in this book.

So get ready. I am going to show you professional, no-holds-barred job-hunting techniques that are little known outside the personnel placement industry. Many of these techniques are being published for the first time. I will instruct you on how to plan your job-hunting campaign over a realistic period of time. I will tell you, for each phase of your campaign and for each technique, exactly what results you can expect. I will explain psychological testing and tell you how to do well when testing is a requirement. I will show you how to establish your overall career objective and how to pick your next job for maximum impact on your career. I will assist you in developing a superior resume and guide you in using it effectively. I will teach you every method of getting job interviews, instruct you in how to train for them, and make you an expert interviewee. I will detail the secrets of how to make use of headhunters, personnel managers, hiring executives, and other "players" you will meet during your campaign. I will show you how to maintain control of the hiring situation until you get the superior job that you want. In sum, I will describe every important aspect of job hunting that you must know in order to succeed.

A job campaign is like business itself. Your potential employer is the customer. You are the product. Other executives who are seeking the same job are your competition. In this book you will learn how to satisfy your customer and beat the competition. You will learn how to consistently find superior jobs.

William A. Cohen

Contents

	Introduction	**1**
1	Why Developing a Positive Mental Attitude is Crucial and How to Do It at Once	**3**
2	How to Define and Reach Your Personal Professional Objectives	**9**
3	How to Plan Your Job Campaign	**16**
4	How to Develop a Superior Resume	**27**
5	Personal Sales Letters: The Number-One Method of Getting a Job	**35**
6	How to Get Interviews Through Answering Advertisements	**58**
7	How to Become Expert at Using the Phone to Get Interviews	**74**
8	How to Advertise Yourself	**82**
9	How to Get a Job Through a Corporate Headhunter	**91**
10	How to Find a Superior Job in Secret	**99**
11	The Advantages of Being Unemployed	**105**
12	How to Use Friends Effectively in Your Campaign	**108**
13	The Concentration Strategy	**113**
14	Strategies for a Tough Job Market	**119**
15	How to Interview Effectively	**128**
16	How to Beat Psychological Tests	**146**
17	How to Get a Superior Job After Leaving the Service	**151**
18	How to Make the Personnel Manager an Ally Instead of an Adversary	**161**
19	How to Insure That You Have Superior Reference Checks	**166**
20	How to Negotiate a Significant Salary Increase	**170**
21	Job Counseling Services: When and How to Use Them	**177**
22	Successful Executive Job Campaigns	**182**
23	Some Questions Frequently Asked About Getting a Superior Job	**187**
24	It's Up to You	**193**
	Index	**194**

Introduction

Job finding is one of the most important executive skills. It is essential because even the best executives are liable, through no fault of their own, to be laid off, fired, or otherwise forced to resign. Even more important, job-hunting skills can give executives self-confidence and freedom of action on the job. No manager or profesional who must choose between remaining at a job or starving can perform to maximum potential. Such executives will be under constant pressure to conform to a company image and to make decisions that may be more popular than wise. At the very least, they will be inhibited from presenting their views forcefully because of fear of endangering their jobs. To quote Peter Drucker in his book *Management: Tasks, Responsibilities, Practices,* "Living in fear of loss of job and income is incompatible with taking responsibility for job and work group, for output and performance."

Mastering the job-hunting techniques in this book will not only get you a better job, it will make you a better executive. You should read the Prefaces, Introduction, and Chapters 1 through 3 at once so that you can get started on your job campaign. They will give you a bird's-eye view of what your campaign will consist of, what it will cost, how long it will take, and how much effort it will require. Chapter 1 shows you why developing a positive mental attitude is crucial to your campaign and why you must do it as soon as possible. This chapter is important if you are currently unemployed, and even more important if you have been unemployed for any period of time. (If you have been unemployed for a while, you should start your campaign anew, as I have described in the book.) Chapter 2 tells you how to define and reach your personal professional objectives. Until you have defined your job objectives precisely, you will not be able to make much progress. Chapter 3 outlines your campaign plan and shows you how to develop a road map to reach your goal. When you have completed Chapter 3 and laid out your plan, you will know what you want and exactly where you are and where you are going at any point during your campaign.

Chapters 4 through 13 will enable you to get interviews, and lots of them. The interview is an essential intermediate objective. You will get job offers only through interviewing. Therefore, don't overlook any of the methods described in these chapters. Integrate them into your campaign and use them all. Once you have developed a superior resume, your primary means of generating interviews will be the personal sales letters described in Chapter 5. This method, by itself, has greater potential than any other to generate interviews and get superior job offers. Chapter 10 is of great help if you are still employed. If you are not now employed, concentrate on Chapter 11.

Chapter 14 is a collection of powerful strategies for use in a tough job market when you must pull out all stops in order to succeed. This chapter will also give you ideas to enable you to create your own tough-job-market strategies.

Study Chapters 15, 16, 18, 19, and 20 *before* going in for your first interview. The secrets contained in these chapters will enable you to interview well and will make you an outstanding candidate for any job for which you are qualified. If you have recently left the service or are anticipating doing so in the near future, you should read Chapter 17 immediately after Chapter 3.

Chapter 21 not only discusses the pros and cons of using job counseling services. It will help you to know when it may be in your interest to use such services and when it may actually hurt your campaign.

Read Chapters 22, 23, and 24 whenever you can spare a few minutes from your planned campaign.

In summary, this book was written with two objectives in mind: (1) to enable you to get a superior job at a significant increase in salary within a reasonable period of time (usually ten weeks or less), and (2) to free you from all fear in the future about your ability to get any job for which you are qualified.

1

Why Developing a Positive Mental Attitude Is Crucial and How to Do It at Once

The Importance of a Positive Mental Attitude in Job Hunting

Whether you are currently unemployed or secure in your job, a positive mental attitude is critical in job hunting. Your mental attitude will make a difference in how soon you find a job, what kind of job you are offered, and how much compensation you receive. Even if you follow all the advanced techniques explained in this book, you will be wasting your time in job interviews unless you have the right mental attitude. But if you enter every interview with a positive attitude, you will receive job offers that you never dreamed possible.

Now some of you reading this will say, "I'm not interested in any mental attitude hocus pocus." Let me tell you about George Y., a petroleum engineer whose positive mental attitude got him a job offer when there wasn't even an opening. Through various techniques that I will explain in later chapters, George was able to speak on the phone to the divisional vice president of a large, independent petroleum producer. The vice president, impressed by George's positive personality and attitude, invited him in for a talk, even though "the only opening we have now is for a geologist."

George maintained his positive mental attitude throughout a long interview. Two weeks later he was invited back to "meet some of the boys." Not once was a job mentioned, and not once did George ask. But he maintained his positive attitude and demonstrated his natural enthusiasm for petroleum work and his interest in the company he was "visiting." Several days later George received a job offer. The company had decided that it needed a petroleum engineer more than it needed a geologist. What really happened, of course, was that management decided that a positive fellow like George was too good to pass up.

Be Prepared for the Hard Knocks of Job Hunting

No matter how good you are or what you have done in the past, you are going to suffer some hard knocks during your job-hunting campaign. Not all prospective employers (PEs) are going to like you, appreciate your talents, or understand your accomplishments, just as you are not going to like or appreciate every PE you meet. But sometime during your campaign you will meet a PE whom you like very much. You will think yourself a perfect match for the company and feel that you will be able to do wonders for it. You will be disappointed if you do not receive a job offer. Be ready for such temporary setbacks. Like a good marriage, the perfect job match comes when both parties are totally convinced. You must be sure that it is an outstanding opportunity, and the company must be sure that you will do a superb job. In the interim you must maintain your positive mental attitude. Here's how to do it.

After a really super interview that you are certain will lead to an offer, get ready for the next interview with the next company. Tell yourself that you are going to have such a great interview that you will receive another offer to compare with the first. In fact, I want you to sit back and actually visualize yourself getting a telephone call from the first company with the offer. Imagine the exact words that will be said to you, as well as your reply. Now do the same thing with the coming interview. Visualize the interview going extremely well and the PE of the second company saying, "You'll do a great job with our company and we must have you. Here is our offer." Psychologists have found that this technique is remarkably successful. You will find that it works wonders in helping to give you a winning attitude. This technique is called mental visualization or mental rehearsal, and I'll be telling you more about research on executives who have used this technique successfully, as described in *The Wall Street Journal*.

Now answer additional advertisements, as explained in Chapter 6. See if you can raise your response-to-interview ratio by writing the "perfect" response. Make more telephone calls, following the telephone training program discussed in Chapter 7. Try to beat your old record of number of calls to interviews. If it fits in with your campaign plan, send out additional sales letters or follow-up sales letters. Go over your old letter to iron out any mistakes. Be confident that in the end you will achieve your objective and capture a truly superior job.

How to Use Your Resume to Develop a Positive Attitude

Even after you have developed a superior resume and are well into your job campaign, you should read over your resume every morning and evening. There are two reasons for rereading your resume so many times. First, as your campaign develops and you begin to interview, important items that you have forgotten will come to light. You will want to include them in your resume. Second, by reading about your strong experiences, background, and accomplishments you will realize just what a tremendous catch you are.

You really have a lot to offer. You are unique! You have a unique set of qualifications stemming from years of work or service at any number of vocations and avocations. As you reread your accomplishments, you will realize that by finding a superior job, you are rendering a service not only to yourself but also to that company fortunate enough to hire you. This knowledge will assist you in maintaining a positive mental attitude as you attend to everyday tasks and will ultimately lead to your accepting that superior position.

How to Avoid Negative Feelings During Interviews

The only way to avoid negative feelings during interviews is to maintain positive ones. It is a fact that you cannot have both negative and positive thoughts at the same time. Before you interview get to know both yourself and your PE. Find out everything you can about the job, the company, and the people you will meet. Think about how you would act in the job. Imagine yourself in the environment of that company. Picture yourself as an executive there. The more you know about the company and the more you can imagine yourself working there, the less nervous you will be and the more positive an image you will project.

During your first few interviews you may still feel some nervousness. Don't worry about it. It will lessen with time. During the next few interviews you will find yourself improving your skill. You will get better and better. In fact, many job hunters end up enjoying interviewing so much that they miss it once they have accepted a position. They enjoy interviewing because it gives them a chance to show off certain "people skills" they have developed. It also gives them an opportunity to meet new people in their profession and learn about their industry and specialty. Above all, many job hunters enjoy the challenge of interviewing, of trying to get a PE to make them a job offer.

You may not believe it now, but you too may enjoy interviewing. In fact, you may like it too much. So a word of caution. Never become so overconfident or cocky in your interviews that you lose sight of your main purpose: to find a superior job.

The Secret of Dealing from Strength in a Job Campaign

On several occasions I have resigned from one job before beginning to search for another. But I have never accepted a new job without a significant salary increase. One PE even commented during an interview: "Bill, I know you are unemployed, yet you act as if you had a million dollars. What's your secret?" My secret, which enables me to deal from strength under any circumstances, is this: I know my own strengths. I spend a considerable amount of time working on my resume, making sure I have written down every useful and appropriate bit of experience in my background. Knowing my strengths and remembering my accomplishments gives me tremendous self-confidence. I know that I am a unique individual who has much to offer to the company that hires me. I also know my job goal. I know exactly what position I want—the industry, the kind of company, the location, and the compensation. Because I know my own strengths and experience, I am confident that I can do an outstanding job in the position I have decided upon.

I know the company I am interviewing with. I have studied the company's history, products, and financial position. I know the backgrounds of some of the leading executives, including, if possible, the executive I am interviewing with. I probably even know why this company is seeking my services. I make it my business to learn as much as I can before the interview. As a result, I sometimes know as much about the company, in a general way, as the executive who is doing the interviewing. Finally, I know what the outcome of my campaign will be. I have seen other executives find superior jobs, and I know that I am at least as good in my own field and am confident of my ability to find a superior job.

By the time you complete this book, you will be able to use my secret too.

How Ray S. Got a Superior Job
Through a Positive Mental Attitude

Ray S. was a young Air Force officer who completed his obligatory service and sought a job as an engineer with an aircraft company. Ray considered his own background. He had a bachelor's degree in engineering from a respectable school. He had four years' experience as an engineer in the Air Force, where he had performed as a project manager and was responsible for the development of aircraft subsystems exceeding $2 million per year. Ray had done very well in directing these government programs and had been commended by his supervisor.

Before beginning his campaign, Ray wrote down everything he had done during this period; after a few days he had several pages of notes. By this time he really knew his strengths. Next, Ray began to think about his goal. He knew he wanted to work for an aircraft company. Because his background was entirely in project management, and because he both enjoyed and excelled at this type of work, Ray decided to pursue it as a career. He began to investigate several aircraft companies. He discovered very quickly that his limited experience made it difficult to move into the kind of job he wanted, given the recessionary climate of the aerospace industry at the time.

Ray did not give up. He learned of a company in a foreign country that was seeking American expertise in building up its aerospace capabilities. The company offered the type of position he sought at a higher salary than he had expected. Ray now had a fully defined job goal. To prepare himself, he studied the company and read up on the country. By the day of the interview Ray was ready. He knew that his campaign would be successful whether this particular company hired him or not. He also knew that he would do well in the interview. He was self-confident and had a positive mental attitude.

It is not remarkable that Ray S. was hired. What is remarkable is that he managed to secure a position a level higher than 80 percent of the other American engineers who were hired, despite the fact that they had from 2 to 25 years more experience than Ray.

Your Ability to Sell Yourself Through Your Attitude

Job hunting is a sales position. You are the product. Your PE is your customer. Other job hunters seeking the same job are your competition. In this book you will find every tool you need to satisfy your customer and beat the competition. But these tools will be of no value unless you have a positive mental attitude. Have you ever seen a successful salesman with a negative attitude? Of course not. The same is true for the successful job hunter. A positive mental attitude will attract job offers. A negative mental attitude—expressing negative feelings or telling hard-luck stories to a PE—will get you only the most undesirable job situations. Like the successful salesman, you should always fill your mind with positive thoughts. A positive mental attitude is the key to selling yourself successfully to a PE.

Some of these points bear repeating:

1. To be prepared for the hard knocks of job hunting:
    After one interview, immediately start to prepare for the next.
    After a successful interview, answer additional advertisements and try to write the perfect response.
    As you are waiting for the offer you know will come, make more telephone calls as explained in the TTP and try to beat your old record of number of calls to interviews.
    Keep sending out your sales letters and follow-up letters in accordance with your campaign plan. Always keep trying to make them better.
    Know that in the end you will secure a truly superior job.
2. Use your resume to develop a positive mental attitude.
3. Use my secret to deal always from strength.
    Know your own strengths.
    Decide on your goals.
    Know the company you are going to interview with.
    Know that the outcome of your campaign will be successful as it has been for others.
4. Remember that to be a successful job hunter, you must be able to sell yourself. This book will show you how, but a positive mental attitude is essential.

2

How to Define and Reach Your Personal Professional Objectives

You Can't Get a Job Until You Know the Job You Want

Many job hunters start their campaigns with only the fuzziest notion of the kind of job they want. Some think this is an advantage: if they keep "all their options open," they might get a job that they would otherwise have overlooked. Don't make this mistake! True, as your campaign progresses your job goal will become clearer. But you can lose job offers if you aren't specific about the job you seek, right from the start.

PEs are interested in men and women who know their own minds and know what they want in life. They are much less interested in suggesting opportunities to you or trying to help you find something of interest on the remote possibility that you might be qualified. Further, PEs are interested in you because of expertise you are offering in an area which they feel they are currently lacking. This might be in sales, it might be in finance, or it might be in general management. Anything you say that does not reinforce your image as the best candidate for the job will work to your disadvantage. Even if you speak ten languages, this skill will only blur your image if it is not directly related to the position you are seeking. Further, in a job campaign, time—your most important resource—is limited. To be successful, you must concentrate your efforts on developing a single well-defined opportunity. You cannot afford to dissipate your energies by going after many different job goals simultaneously.

Finally, you cannot plan steps toward reaching a job goal until you decide exactly what that job goal is. There is one exception to this rule. Despite the fact that you have aimed at a single type of job and have prepared your job campaign accordingly, occasionally a PE will single out an accomplishment in your resume and ask whether you would be interested in a position other than the one you are seeking. You will have to evaluate such an opportunity on its own merits. Even so, you should never establish more than one precisely defined goal at the start or allow a singular interest by one PE to redirect your entire job campaign. In short, spend some time deciding what you want, then go after that specific goal.

How to Establish Your Overall Career Goal

If you are like many executives, your next job is not the last job you will hold. It is one more milestone in your career. Before you can establish a milestone goal, you must establish an overall career goal. Each person's professional career goal will differ. A company president may aspire to be president of a much larger company, president of a company in another industry, or an entrepreneur-president; the executive may even want to leave management entirely and go into something else.

Regardless of your function or job level, you must establish an overall professional career goal. Once you do, you can begin thinking about what jobs you must have as milestones in order to achieve your overall career goal. Then you can focus on the job you want as your next intermediate goal and concentrate your resources on attaining it.

Many unemployed job hunters think that they can easily get a job if only they take a step down. This is a mistake. In fact, it is generally easier to take another step up than to go backward. If you try to get a job on a lower level or for less money, your PE will feel that there must be something wrong and will assume that if you have once worked at a higher level you will not be happy working at a lower one. Further, your PE will be afraid that you will leave the first time you are offered a job at your proper level.

Going backward is an uphill battle. Don't try to fight it. You should always seek a job that builds on what you have done before, so that your career proceeds in a logical sequence. If you have not done this in the past, the time to start is now.

The Easiest Job to Get

What type of job is the easiest to get? The easiest job to get is one in your present industry, in an identical or similar function to the one you now perform, and in the same or a similar-size company. It is a job at the same level as or one level higher than the one at which you are now working, at a salary 5 to 20 percent higher than what you are presently earning. For a quick and relatively easy job hunt, you must take these five factors into consideration. A sixth factor, geographical location, you may or may not want to consider in your job-hunting campaign.

This does not mean that you cannot immediately increase your present salary by 25 percent or more, change industries or functions, go from a large company to a small one (or vice versa), move to a desirable geographical location, or jump several levels in responsibility. However, if any or all of these objectives are part of your job goal, you should recognize that they will make your search more difficult than "the easiest job to get." You will have to allow for a longer and more difficult campaign.

How to Define Your Specific Job Objectives

You have established an overall professional career goal and identified job position steps that will take you there. You are now ready to precisely define the job you will be seeking, a position that will also be the next step toward reaching your overall career goal.

Industry

Do your overall career plans call for you to "make it" in the industry in which you are presently working, or must you make a change? Generally, it is easier to get a job in the industry in which you were most recently employed, even during a recession, because any industry always needs good people, even if that industry is in a recessionary mode, or maybe especially then. Your job is to communicate your outstanding qualifications better than your competitors. If you make an industry change during a recession, you will frequently find that much of your competition has moved with you. Unless you have prior experience in the industry or are currently employed in it, you will not have a real advantage over the competition. The same, of course, holds true even if there is no recession.

Those of your competitors seeking positions in the same industry that are already working in it have the advantage.

What if your career plans give you no choice? You have decided that you need experience in another industry in order to progress, or other factors have led you to the decision to make a career outside of the industry in which you are presently employed regardless of the increased difficulty in getting a job. Then your campaign must be organized to stress your functional accomplishments, and industry should be de-emphasized. You should define exactly what industry you are going after and you should learn everything about that industry that you possibly can. If you have the time to take courses before beginning your campaign, by all means take them. Successful completion will provide additional support for an industry switch. Read all the books you can and pick up the buzzwords. Talk with friends or former classmates who are currently working in the industry. You can change industries successfully if you plan the change carefully and allow yourself additional time for your campaign.

Company

It's easier to get a position with the same type and size of company as the one you are presently working for. However, changing the type of company is easier than changing industry. Any prior experience in the type of company you are seeking will make your path much smoother, provided you use the techniques I discuss elsewhere in this book. So if you are now with a small company and have at one time been with a much larger one (or vice versa), you will probably have little trouble getting back in. If you have not had prior experience, your task will be a little more difficult.

In all your communications with potential employers, you should stress both the similarity of work and the similarity of positions. You should accentuate the positive, withholding information about major company differences until the interview. Before the interview you are not obligated to reveal any information about present or past employers that does not support your case. One way of doing this (and I will explain in more detail later) is simply to omit the company name from information you supply before an interview. Use descriptive terms such as "a prestigious consulting company," "a well-known finance company," "an important aerospace firm," or "one of America's leading pharmaceuticals houses." If you are asked over the telephone for names, say that for security reasons you prefer to withhold this information until mutual interest has been established. Once that interest has been established, you will almost always be required to give detailed background data.

Function

Even if you have had prior experience, you should give a great deal of thought before attempting a change function. It is one of the most difficult career changes to pull off, because it raises serious questions in the mind of your PE. Why are you changing? If you have the experience and talent in the function you are seeking, why doesn't your present employer give you an opportunity in that area?

If you decide to change functions, you should marshal every accomplishment and experience in your background for support. You must also be prepared to explain why you want to change. Obviously answers such as "I thought I'd give it a try" or "I want to get experience in more than one functional area so that I can break into general management" will kill any chance you may have had. So you must spend extra time preparing for the interview to make sure you have an argument that will be acceptable to your PE.

Level

Changing levels is one area where you can jump big, within certain limits. These limits are that your last job should appear to lead into the new job you are seeking. For support you can use one or more of the following:

Salary level
References (level and type)
Title of individual you currently report to
Number of people you currently supervise
Responsibility (quantified in dollars)
Title of your present job

You should be able to find some support in these six factors. For example, you can probably drum up some high-level references (company president, congressman, high-ranking military officer) from your past. You should be able to figure out your responsibilities in dollars—the dollar value of the programs you are working on, annual sales, dollar value of the acquisitions you analyzed and recommended, or whatever. If you haven't done this before, the total value will probably amaze you. If your current title does not reflect your present responsibilities, make it so. I am not recommending that you promote yourself to a company officership. However, if your company gives a title such as "engineer" to everyone from a new hire on through the ranks, you should state your title according to the function you are actually fulfilling: project engineer, program manager, chief engineer, and so on.

Do not volunteer any information that does not offer support for the job level you are seeking. As a rule, you should withhold exact information on references and salary until final negotiations. You can usually sidestep any other questions you would like to avoid by controlling the interview, as outlined in Chapter 15.

When you get down to final negotiations, you will have to furnish references, and you may be forced into stating your last salary. Make certain your references are of the same seniority as or higher than the position you will report to. You will do nothing to help your cause if you are looking for a position in top management and offer as a reference a first-line supervisor. A cardinal rule is to avoid discussing salary at all; if you must, use the techniques outlined in Chapter 20. Make certain that the salary fits in with other job information you have given and is at most 20 to 30 percent lower than the anticipated salary of the position you are seeking. If you are shooting for even bigger gains, read on.

Compensation

Whether you are employed are not, it is always easier to take a jump up in salary, barring a major depression. If your goal is to make a really big jump in salary, do not tell any PE your present salary level. (The reasons are explained in detail elsewhere in this book.) You should negotiate salary on the basis of what the new position merits, not what you have made previously. Even if your goal is a moderate increase, you should follow this principle. If for any reason you are forced into revealing your former salary, be certain to include bonus, automobile, stock options, and other fringes as part of the total compensation package.

Once you have released salary information about yourself to a PE, you should recognize that you probably limited yourself to a 10 to 20 percent increase. But there are exceptions to this rule, and you are still free to try to negotiate whatever compensation you want. As a headhunter, I once watched a young oil landsman who was in great demand negotiate himself a 66 percent increase in salary. I also witnessed a much-needed professional turn down a 300 percent increase over what he had been making. In each case, the PE knew the candidate's compensation level. But these cases are exceptions to what is most definitely the norm.

Geographical Location

Geographical location, unlike the other five factors, is rarely negotiated. Still, it is an important part of your job objective, and you must give it some thought. If you are willing to go anywhere in the world to meet the other parts of your objective, that is fine. If you are not, you should decide on location before you get started. If you are after a certain location and none other, you will have to limit the target companies you select for your campaign. There is no point sending out sales letters to companies in the East when you know that you will accept a new position only in Arizona. I needn't add that certain garden spots are almost impossible to capture because of incredible competition, coupled with low demand. A little investigation at the beginning can save you much time and effort.

You won't need to bring up the subject of geographical location to your PE. Either the location will be self-evident or at some point the PE will say, "Would you consider an assignment in . . . ?" You should know the answer to this question before you begin your campaign.

In this chapter, we have discussed:

Why you can't get a job until you decide what kind of job you want
How and why you must establish your overall career objective
How your next job is tied in with your present job
The easiest job to get
How to pick industry, company, function, level, compensation, and
    geographical location

After studying this chapter, sit down and decide on your job objective in terms of the factors we have discussed. Then write down a complete description on the form shown in Figure 1.

Figure 1. My next job position.

Function _____
Level of responsibility _____
Position will report to _____
Responsibilities _____

_____

Title _____
Salary range _____
Industry _____
Type of company _____
Geographical location _____

3

How to Plan
Your Job Campaign

Your Campaign Plan Is Your Road Map to Success

Once you have decided on the kind of job you want, you face the problem of getting from where you are now to the point where you accept the offer of a superior job. If you were traveling to a place you had never been to before, you would get there most easily and most expeditiously by using a road map. In going from your present job (or unemployment) to the position of your choice, you will also use a road map. This road map is the campaign plan.

The campaign plan for job hunting will guide you to logical and effective courses of action, just as other types of plans guide you in reaching objectives on the job. The campaign plan for job hunting has been designed to enable you to get the job you want in the shortest possible time. Do not embark on a job campaign without first developing a plan as outlined in this chapter. If you do, you will remain on your job hunt longer and will limit the range of jobs available to you.

Any job campaign consists of three phases:

1. The preinterview phase
2. The interview phase
3. The postinterview phase

Note that the wording clearly emphasizes the interview. This is done to focus you on your real objective for each phase. Your initial objective is to get the interview. You won't be in a position to get an offer until you do. Your next objective (once you've been given the opportunity to interview) is to handle the interview successfully. Successful interviewing means that you have sold the PE on hiring your services, which puts you in a position to get the job offer. Your final objective is to negotiate that offer success- fully.

Every campaign is different, reflecting different job objectives as well as different professional career goals. Using the outlines and campaign plan detailed in this chapter, you must tailor your campaign to your particular situation.

The Preinterview Phase of Your Campaign

Preparing Your Resume

It will take you two to three days (assuming eight hours per day) to get all your materials together and write your resume, as I will instruct you in Chapter 4. Once you do, you will have all the data you need to:

- Write sales letters with at least five major accomplishments in support of your job objective.
- Prepare responses to advertisements that are right on target with the requirements listed in the ad.
- Prepare special resumes of your experiences that slant your accomplishments to the requirements of the job.

Writing Sales Letters

It will take you two to four days to write sales letters that support your job objectives and mail them to both PEs and executive recruiters.

Printing Sales Letters

Printing your sales letters depends on your printer. This can take up to two weeks, because you will need to order specially printed stationery before your sales letter is added from a soft plate. If you shop around a little, you should be able to find a printer who can do the job in a week or less.

Obtaining Mailing Lists

You should start with a mailing list of 1,000 companies, any one of which you would be prepared to work for if other aspects of the job met your requirements. (I'll tell you later in the book how to develop your list.) You do not need to know everything about these companies. Just make sure they are all on target. For example, if you are looking only for a large company, you shouldn't have any small companies on your list. You will also need a similar list of executive recruiters. Preparing these lists can take several days of somewhat tedious work.

Mailing Sales Letters

Mailing sales letters includes the following mundane, but necessary chores: typing your name and address on both sales letters and envelopes, signing the letters, sealing and stamping the envelopes, and mailing. If you do these tasks yourself, you will spend about 5 hours per 100 letters. Therefore, if you mail sales letters to 1,000 companies and 500 executive recruiters, you can estimate 75 hours of work, or roughly nine days to complete this part of the job. This points out vividly the advantages of getting some family assistance if possible, or even hiring some part-time secretarial help.

Answering Advertisements

Begin to collect job advertisements the day you decide to look for a job, but don't start responding until you get your sales letters out. More than likely, you will not start answering ads until the beginning of the third week. Don't worry about this "lost time." As explained fully in Chapter 6, the fact that you answer ads late is not a disadvantage.

Practicing the Telephone Training Program

After you have caught up on your ad answering and have it under control, start your telephone training program (TTP), as outlined in Chapter 7. You should maintain the program for two weeks, or as long as it takes you to become comfortable and proficient in speaking with PE-related people on the telephone. Shoot for talking with 20 executives (not their secretaries) per day. Try to get at least one interview a day in this fashion. If you follow this regime every weekday for two weeks, you will have talked with 200 executives; and if you have done it right, you will have lined up at least ten interviews.

Meeting with Employment Agencies and Headhunters

Start setting up interviews with employment agencies and headhunters at the same time you begin your TTP. Do not interview with more than five agencies unless it is for a specific job. Otherwise, your resume is likely to be scattered throughout the job market. Like most products that appear to be in great supply, you will not have the image of being in much demand.

Keeping Records of Sales Letter Results

Your recordkeeping will begin with the receipt of "rejects" about one to two weeks after you mail your first batch of sales letters. You will use these records to update your list of names (several executives will have resigned, retired, or been fired or transferred), and to start building a new mailing list of executives for a second mailing. Your records will show you how effective your sales letters are and whether you should revise them before your next mailing.

Writing the Second Sales Letter

You should write your second sales letter about three weeks after your first mailing. If you received good results with your first letter, you will need to make only minor adjustments. If the results were poor, you may have to make major alterations. You should not hesitate to do this. The factor that distinguishes good from poor results is not replies, but interviews (see Chapter 5). You should plan on about two days to write a new sales letter.

Printing the Second Letter

You should have the second sales letter printed just as you did the first.

Mailing the Second Letter

You will not need to spend a lot of time compiling a new mailing list, since day-to-day recordkeeping has updated your initial list. Eliminate those companies on your list that have contacted you to set up an interview. Keep track of your second sales letter results, as you did your first, in case an additional mailing is required.

Setting Up Interviews

You will begin to set up interviews generated by sales letters about three weeks after your first mailing. Invitations will come from the executive you have sent the sales letter to as well as from personnel department people and staff personnel. The majority of invitations will come by telephone. This is one reason the TTP is so important. Most executives will want to talk with you by phone before seeing you, especially if the interview requires travel at the PE's expense.

You should continue to set up interviews until you get and accept a superior job offer. You can always cancel an interview. It is much more difficult to arrange an interview after you have told a PE that you are declining because you expect a job offer. You may then have to answer embarrassing questions about why the offer was not extended. Of course, after you interview and have made a "sale," you are free to say you are expecting another offer or have received one.

Certain actions, such as contacting friends, are discussed in later chapters. These alternative ways of getting interviews are important to your campaign and should be integrated into your overall plan.

The Interview Phase of Your Campaign

Preparing for the Interview

Once you have an interview lined up, you should learn everything possible about the hiring executive, the company, and its products. You should also develop a list of questions to ask and prep yourself for questions that are likely to be asked of you. Plan on several hours of preparation for each face-to-face interview that you schedule. One successful candidate I know spent two weeks in preparation. It resulted in an $80,000 a year offer—a 100 percent increase over his former salary—even though he was out of work at the time.

You will accept every interview offered, unless you are offered so many that time limitations force you to pick and choose. Even if you are pressed for time, you should try to make every single interview you can, even if you must schedule two interviews a day. Remember, interviews and interviews alone will get you job offers. Also, if you apply yourself, you will get better with every interview. By the end of your campaign you will be getting job offers you would not have received when you first started interviewing. Finally, you will learn more about the job and whether you really want it from the interview than from any other source (short of actually working for the company).

The Postinterview Phase of Your Campaign

Writing the Postinterview Letter

The postinterview letter is written and mailed one day after the interview. Plan on spending several hours getting this letter just right. Unless you are one of the lucky job hunters who are deluged by interviews, you should have no problem getting an outstanding postinterview letter written and mailed promptly. You will find instructions on writing this letter in Chapter 15.

Preparing the Special Resume

The special resume is generally prepared after the interview and can be mailed with the postinterview letter if a resume is expected by the PE. In a few cases, generally if the PE must pay your travel expenses, you may have to send out a special resume before the interview. In this case, you will use techniques taught to you elsewhere in the book to obtain all the intelligence you can about the position and base your special resume on this information. It should take you no more than a couple of hours to prepare a special resume, since you have already assembled all the facts and materials you need at the beginning of your campaign.

Negotiating

Negotiations can take much longer than you might imagine, even for middle management positions. This is especially true in large companies or companies that have several different executives involved in the decision-making process. As much as three weeks can elapse between the time that you and the hiring executive come to a meeting of the minds and the time that you receive an offer.

Accepting the Offer

Once a satisfactory offer has been made, do not delay your decision, unless you have several offers that are maturing simultaneously. In that case, it is definitely in your interest to take a good look at all the offers. But don't delay needlessly once you have made your decision.

The Ten-Week Campaign and How to Shorten It

It is difficult to describe the length of an "average" campaign, because there is no such thing. Every job hunter has his own objectives which he has defined, and every job-hunting executive's situation is different. However, in very general terms, the campaign detailed in this chapter is designed to last approximately ten weeks, from start to acceptance of the offer. This allows extra time for consideration of the offer, delays by the PE, and administrative tasks such as printing and typing. You can shorten the ten-week campaign by reducing the time for subcontracted tasks such as printing, having someone else do your typing, or working more than eight hours a day on your campaign. Another way to shorten the time is not to set excessively high requirements as part of your job objective.

If you are currently employed, you will not be able to spend even eight hours a day on your campaign, or you may need to campaign in secret. You must work harder than the unemployed executive. Work on your campaign at night or on weekends. Get someone else to do your typing. Unless you can take a vacation, you will not be able to work on the TTP. Also, you may have difficulty setting up interviews or meetings with employment agencies.

Figure 2 represents a completed campaign plan for an unemployed job hunter who is not campaigning in secret and who is putting in eight hours every day plus weekends on the campaign. Figure 3 is a completed campaign plan for an employed job hunter campaigning in secret. It assumes that typing is done by someone else and that interviews will be scheduled for after hours or on weekends. Using these two examples, design your own job campaign plan. Figure 4 is a blank campaign form to enable you to do so.

Once you have put your campaign plan into action, you will need to adjust your plan. Certain tasks may take you less time than you planned; other tasks may take longer or may have to be repeated. In addition, responses to your sales letters and answers to advertisements will not all arrive at the same time. You may receive an offer from one company at the same time as your interview with another company. You should adjust your plan accordingly. Finally, you may find yourself so successful in some phase of your campaign (for example, getting more interviews than you can handle) that good sense dictates holding other campaign tasks in abeyance.

(text continues on page 26)

Figure 2. Campaign plan for an unemployed job hunter.

WEEK	PHASE I								PHASE II	PHASE III
	1	2	3	4	5	6	7	8	9	10
Prepare resume	↑									
Write initial sales letters	↑									
Print initial sales letters		↑								
Develop mailing lists		↑								
Type addresses and mail sales letters		↑								
Answer advertisements								↑		
Telephone training program					↑					
Employment agency interviews					↑					
Talk to friends					↑					
Write second sales letters					↑					
Print second sales letters						↑				
Type addresses and mail second sales letters							↑			
Set up interviews									↑	
Interviews									↑	
Write and send postinterview letter/resume										↑
Negotiations										↑
Offer acceptance										↑

Figure 3. Campaign plan for an employed job hunter.

WEEK	1	2	3	4	5	6	7	8	9	10
Prepare resume	↑									
Write initial sales letters	—	↑								
Set up number to receive telephone calls	—	↑								
Set up address to receive letters	—	↑								
Print initial sales letters		—	↑							
Develop mailing lists		—	↑							
Type addresses and mail sales letters			↑							
Break "blind" advertisements			—	—	—	—	↑			
Answer advertisements			—	—	—	—	—	↑		
Employment agency interviews			—	—	—	—	↑			
Talk to friends			—	—	—	—	↑			
Write second sales letters						↑				
Print second sales letters						—	↑			
Type addresses and mail second sales letters							—	↑		
Set up interviews						—	—	—	↑	
Interviews						—	—	—	↑	
Write and send postinterview letter/resume						—	—	—	—	↑
Negotiations						—	—	—	—	↑
Offer acceptance										↑

PHASE   I   II   III

Figure 4. Your job campaign plan.

PHASE

WEEK	1	2	3	4	5	6	7	8	9	10

What Your Campaign Will Cost

In addition to living expenses, your job campaign will require outlays for printing, phone calls, postage, local travel, and any services you engage. Generally, your PE will pick up travel-plus expenses for interviews out of your local area.

You should conserve your funds, but do not be afraid to spend money when it is important. For example, do not skimp on printing costs by purchasing cheap stationery or mediocre printing. Until the interview your sales letter is the only thing a PE has that directly represents you. (Stationery styles and printing are described in detail in Chapter 5.) Go first class. Don't be afraid to spend the money. The same holds true for your personal appearance. Money invested in appearance for an interview is money well spent.

Figure 5 is a form for estimating your campaign costs. Since prices for printing and other services will vary widely from one part of the country to another, I have included two columns in the figure. The first shows my estimates. Use the blank second column to fill in your estimates, according to conditions in your area.

Finding a superior job will cost money. Of course, a single paycheck can pay back your entire investment. Still, you should consider estimated costs as an important part of your overall campaign plan and fill out the cost form after you have designed your campaign plan in Figure 4.

Figure 5. Estimated campaign costs.

Printing of 2,000 sales letters with letterheads and envelopes to PEs	$150	
Printing of 500 sales letters with letterheads and envelopes to executive recruiters	100	
First-class postage for 2,500 letters	500	
Telephone calls: 300 local plus 20 long distance	200	
Local travel	100	
Haircuts, dry cleaning, and other personal expenses	100	
Typing services	100	

4

How to Develop
a Superior Resume

Developing your resume is the first action item in your job campaign. It comes first because it is the foundation of your job-hunting endeavor. If you get your resume right at the foundation stage, you can save considerable time later. So before you are tempted to dust off your resume from several years back and add a couple of lines, read this chapter.

Why a Professional Resume Writer
Should Not Do Your Resume

Many executive job hunters recognize that the resume is important to their campaign, but they do not want to take the time to develop the superior resume they need. They do a very natural thing. They turn to the professional resume writer. Don't make that mistake. It is essential to your campaign that you prepare your own resume.

To begin with, no one knows you as you know yourself. Even if the professional resume writer spends several hours with you (and most will not), consider how long you have spent with yourself. You cannot remember everything you should during the time you interview with a professional resume writer or complete a questionnaire. Important facts will occur to you later, as your campaign proceeds. Even more important, small items that you considered incidental to your career will assume a more primary role. The professional resume writer, not knowing you as you know yourself and not being a part of your campaign, will fix in concrete at the beginning a resume based on only what he knows about you at that time. No matter how well written, this resume may be useless only days into your campaign.

Every professional resume writer has a particular style, good, bad, or indifferent. You may like the style or not. The point is it is not your style. Most people who read resumes have learned to spot the styles of certain professional resume-writing firms. Inevitably the thought must occur to them that a resume prepared for you, and not by you, indicates a lack of writing ability or a lack of self-confidence in written communication.

In developing your own resume and wording your experiences and accomplishments properly, you will have a chance to think about your career in a logical fashion. You cannot do this if you fill out a form or discuss your background with someone. You cannot do it by reading over what someone else has interpreted your career to be. You must take the time to organize these facts yourself. There is no easier way, but it will be worth the effort. The experience will help you later in writing a sales letter, answering advertisements, and discussing your background on the telephone or in face-to-face interviews.

A professional resume-writing service, whatever it costs, is a misallocation of your financial resources. Remember, any job campaign costs money. Unless you are financially independent and don't need to work, it is important to allocate your financial resources where they do the most good. Hiring someone else to write your resume will waste money that you could spend more profitably elsewhere.

How to Use the Resume Preparation Form

The type of resume that I will show you how to write is not one that many employment counselors would encourage. There is good reason for this. Much of the information commonly put in resumes and subsequently distributed to prospective employers has little bearing not only on whether you will be hired, but on whether you will be invited in for an interview. You cannot attain the first without the second. The sole purpose of sending information to a PE, whether through a resume or an extract, is to obtain an interview. No one will hire you on the basis of a resume alone; you will be hired only on the basis of a face-to-face interview. Therefore, your resume and subsequent sales letters, answers to advertisements, and telephone conversations must be geared to achieving that objective: the interview. That is the kind of resume I will show you how to write.

Figure 6 is a resume preparation form that will assist you in developing

(text continues on page 32)

Figure 6. Resume preparation form.

My Next Job Position
Function _____
Level of responsibility _____
Position will report to _____
Responsibilities _____

_____

Title _____
Salary range _____
Industry _____
Type of company _____
Geographical location _____

Career History
Note: Start with last job. Be as specific as possible. For example, instead of saying, "Conducted a large number of personnel interviews," say, "Conducted 343 personnel interviews."

Company name _____
Dates of employment _____
Type of product or service _____
Annual sales volume _____
Division in which employed _____
Reported to _____
Starting and ending salary _____
Reason for leaving _____
Titles held _____

_____

_____

Job responsibilities
Note: Include budget, number of people reporting to you and titles, responsibilities for equipment and material, and any other quantification of your responsibilities.

_____

_____

_____

Accomplishments

Note: Be specific and quantify all accomplishments. Relate them to sales, profits, or cost savings when possible. List at least five accomplishments for every position you held with this company. For example:

1. Doubled sales of widgets to $1 million per year in one year.
2. Developed and directed bid/no bid systems that saved $50,000 per year.
3. Designed eight widgets that resulted in sales to date of $15 million.
4. Developed cost-accounting system that saved $200,000 per year.
5. Directed development of widget that achieved 25 percent increase in performance with no increase in cost.

_____

_____

_____

_____

Successful Management Recommendations

Note: List recommendations you made on organization, administration, or management that were successfully implemented. For example: "Recommended that R&D department be reorganized for more efficient management of government contracts. As a result, cost overruns decreased by 50 percent and slippages by 12 percent."

_____

_____

_____

_____

Successful Technical Recommendations

Note: List recommendations you made on technical aspects of your job that were successfully implemented. For example: "Recommended bonding a fibrous material with epoxy rather than sewing. As a result, labor for manufacture of this item was reduced by 20 percent."

_____

_____

_____

Promotions and Transfers

Note: List all promotions and transfers of assignment while with the company, along with salary increases and increases in responsibilities.

_____

_____

_____

(*continued*)

Awards, Honors, and Commendations
Note: List every honor, award, or commendation received while with the company. Include verbal commendations if significant. For example: "Commended by company president for 'outstanding management accomplishment' in developing advanced communications subsystem."

_____

_____

_____

Reports, Documents, and Published Articles
Note: Describe reports, documents, or published articles written by you or prepared under your direction. Be sure to describe any special significance attached to a particular item.

_____

_____

_____

Concurrent Away-from-Job Experience and Accomplishments
Note: Describe your "extracurricular" activities during this period. Include social activities, church groups, and club memberships, along with any offices held and accomplishments of particular note.

_____

_____

_____

_____

Repeat all items under "Career History" for every past employer. If you were in the military service, treat every major assignment as a separate company. If your military service was limited to one type of duty (e.g., infantry), consider military service as one company.

Special Qualifications
Note: List special qualifications such as licensed pilot, CPA, registered professional engineer, foreign languages.

_____

_____

_____

Associations
Note: List current associations and professional societies, along with offices held.

_____

_____

_____

NOTE:

The copy on the other side of this sheet should replace the page 31 now in this book.

Accomplishments

Note: Be specific and quantify all accomplishments. Relate them to sales, profits, or cost savings when possible. List at least five accomplishments for every position you held with this company. For example:

1. Doubled sales of widgets to $1 million per year in one year.
2. Developed and directed bid/no bid systems that saved $50,000 per year.
3. Designed eight widgets that resulted in sales to date of $15 million.
4. Developed cost-accounting system that saved $200,000 per year.
5. Directed development of widget that achieved 25 percent increase in performance with no increase in cost.

_____

_____

_____

_____

Successful Management Recommendations

Note: List recommendations you made on organization, administration, or management that were successfully implemented. For example: "Recommended that R&D department be reorganized for more efficient management of government contracts. As a result, cost overruns decreased by 50 percent and slippages by 12 percent."

_____

_____

_____

_____

Successful Technical Recommendations

Note: List recommendations you made on technical aspects of your job that were successfully implemented. For example: "Recommended bonding a fibrous material with epoxy rather than sewing. As a result, labor for manufacture of this item was reduced by 20 percent."

_____

_____

_____

Promotions and Transfers

Note: List all promotions and transfers of assignment while with the company, along with salary increases and increases in responsibilities.

_____

_____

_____

(continued)

Special Accomplishments
Note: List articles, books, copyrights, inventions, and similar accomplishments.

_____
_____
_____

Current Recreational Interests
Note: List hobbies, athletics, and other interests. Make special note of accomplishments—for example, "grand master chess champion."

_____
_____
_____

Professional Training
Note: List courses, dates, and schools for seminars, conferences, training programs, and special courses.

_____
_____
_____

Education
Note: List schools, dates, degrees, majors, and special scholastic honors.

_____
_____
_____

a superior resume. Note that the form begins with the information
contained in "My Next Job Position," which you completed in Chapter 2.
The reason for starting off with this information is to help you to keep your
professional job objective continually in mind as you complete the resume
preparation form. This is not the format you will use to get information to
your PEs. However, it is the best format for recording the information you
will need. You cannot skip this resume preparation step and finish with a
superior resume, just as you cannot perform calculus without first having
prepared yourself with algebra.

The resume preparation form is lengthy and detailed. It should take
you several hours to complete even a sketchy outline. Remember, you
have allotted several days to preparation of a superior resume in your job
campaign plan. Take advantage of this built-in time. You can profitably use
every hour.

The resume preparation form, if properly completed, will insure that all important information needed for your campaign is recalled, documented, and kept together in an organized fashion for immediate use. It will focus your thinking on experiences and accomplishments, both in your career and outside of work, that support your job position objectives. It will increase your self-confidence immeasurably, as you see before you the unique experiences and accomplishments that you alone can offer to a PE. Finally, it will save you a considerable amount of time during your campaign.

The Importance of Special, Short, and Outside-of-Work Assignments

You will find places on the resume preparation form for information about special and short assignments in your career and special experience outside of your career. Such information is frequently overlooked; but it can be vital to your campaign. For example, Douglas M. was an accountant for a small company that manufactured adhesives for the building industry. For about a year, in addition to his normal duties, he represented his department on the company's product evaluation committee. During this period he participated in the evaluation of 32 potential new products. This work, which occupied less than 20 percent of his time during that year and only 4 percent of his total time with the company, was the deciding factor in getting him a position as finance officer with a firm that researched and developed proprietary products for licensing.

Tim O. spent years working as a human factors engineer with a large aerospace company but was faced with a certain layoff. The three months he spent working on ejection seat requirements got him a job as project engineer in charge of the development of a new ejection seat. Special, short, and outside-of-work assignments can be the deciding factor in getting you an interview and getting you a job. Don't overlook them.

Now That You Have a Superior Resume, Don't Send It to Anyone

Your resume will change considerably as your campaign progresses. You will think of new items to add, other accomplishments to emphasize, some statements to delete. You will find this happening right up to the last day of your campaign. How, then, do you handle the hundreds of resumes that must be distributed? Simple—don't. That is, don't send out resumes by hundreds or thousands. In fact, don't send a resume out at all. Instead, send out extracts from your resume tailored to the particular market for your talents. These extracts can be reproduced in large quantities. You will learn exactly how to do this in Chapter 5. Sending out extracts rather than resumes will save you time and money. It will increase your efficiency and effectiveness in getting interviews because you can slant the extracts toward particular job situations much more easily than you can slant the resume itself. You will also avoid "knockout factors," which I'll explain in Chapter 5.

If this is true, when if ever do you send a resume to a PE during your job campaign? There are two situations. The first is when a PE insists on seeing a resume before inviting you for an interview. This may occur when there is travel connected with the interview or when a hiring executive wants to see you but is not fully convinced. In both cases, you should find out everything you can about the potential position before preparing your resume. The situation is analogous to having hooked a fish that hasn't yet swallowed the bait: you could lose him. You will find details on how to gather intelligence about a job later on. The second situation is after the interview. Using the techniques I describe in Chapter 15, you now know a great deal about the job; if you have done your job right, you know far more than any of your competitors. You are now in a position to write an outstanding resume. This is the resume that will help to get you the job.

So begin to develop a superior resume by completing the resume preparation form shown in Figure 6. Filling out the form is one of the most difficult tasks associated with job hunting. But it is well worth your best efforts and will play a major role in the success of your campaign. Remember, this task will not be completed until the very end of your campaign; you will continually update, polish, and reword your resume as you recall additional facts and as your campaign unfolds.

5

Personal Sales Letters: The Number-One Method of Getting a Job

How Personal Sales Letters Lead to Job Offers

Personal sales letters have proved to be the best method of generating interviews that lead to job offers. For this reason, I urge you to emphasize this method above all others in your campaign. A personal sales letter is a one- or two-page document addressed to a PE that describes your outstanding accomplishments in such a way that the PE is convinced you are an exceptional candidate for the job. In this chapter I will show you how to write and package your accomplishments for maximum impact. I promise you that the results of mailing personal sales letters will amaze you; you will be invited in for interviews regardless of the present state of the economy and regardless of your past lack of success in generating interviews.

There are several advantages to letters for getting interviews. The quality of interview derived from a personal sales letter is higher than that derived from any other source, including advertisements, friends, personnel agencies, and the telephone. This means a higher offer-to-interview ratio and less wasted time. Personal sales letters generate more predictable results than other methods of gaining interviews. You will be able to predict roughly how many interviews you will receive for each batch of sales letters you send out. I will discuss this in more detail later.

When you send out personal sales letters, you will have little competition for interviews and little or no competition for the possible job offer. If you respond to an advertisement in *The Wall Street Journal,* for example, you may be competing with 500 or more job hunters for the same position. When you send a personal sales letter, the position may not even be advertised, the company's personnel department may not have been notified, and you may be the only candidate for the job. Imagine presenting your superior qualifications to the hiring executive under these circumstances!

In a personal sales letter you can tailor your experience and accomplishments to the exact specifications (function, level, type of company) of the job you are seeking. When you tailor your response to an advertisement, you are trying to fit someone else's requirements. In the personal sales letter you write to fill *your* requirements.

Using sales letters instead of sending resumes also lets you avoid the problem of "knockout factors." I learned about knockout factors when I was a headhunter. These are factors established by the PE that will prevent you from getting the interview. In other words, if you have one of these factors in your background, you will never be invited in. Further, these factors are frequently foolish and capricious, and they rarely have anything to do with your ability to do the job. They range from the worst of bigotry to such trivia as the part of the country you may be from. To make matters more complicated, you will have no idea what the knockout factors might be in any given job situation. I have never seen a resume that didn't have at least one or two knockout factors that have appeared on some company's list at one time or another.

But the funny thing about knockout factors is that if you do get the interview, they are no longer in force. The reason for this is strictly psychological. No matter how adamant a PE may be about not seeing a candidate with one knockout factor or another, if he does so inadvertently, a powerful force takes over: human like or dislike. The bottom line is that if you have the qualifications and the PE likes you, you will be hired, knockout factor or no. This gets us back to the sales letter. It concentrates on presenting your resources in a brief and forceful manner against a single job objective. Its brevity greatly reduces the chances for some factor—one you may even consider favorable—eliminating you prior to the interview.

Let me give you an example of the effectiveness of sales letters. Jim B. had no experience in job hunting. He had been with the same company for 14 years when he suddenly found himself out of a job. Jim mailed out 1,000 sales letters. Within six weeks he had five firm job offers, all of them at a considerable increase in salary. Even though Jim was out of work, and even though he had not been a supervisor under his former employer, he sought a job only at the supervisory level. All the job offers he received were in this category. Jim accepted the best of the offers. For a month afterward he had to turn down requests for additional interviews.

Why Personal Sales Letters Are So Successful

Obviously, your PE is not sitting and waiting for your personal sales letter to arrive. Why, then, is this technique so successful? At any given time a certain percentage of executives with hiring authority will have personnel needs that must be fulfilled. They may have just begun to think about the problem or may even have extended someone an offer and be awaiting acceptance. It may be a president thinking about replacing a functional vice president, a sales manager recognizing the need for additional salespeople, an operations officer whose production manager has just given two weeks' notice, or a chairman of the board who recognizes that a president will retire imminently because of poor health.

So the recipients of your personal sales letter have their own problems, the exact opposite of yours, which they may or may not have begun to solve. A certain percentage of them will need someone with the skills and experience you possess. The success of your personal sales letter stems from the fact that the product you describe (yourself) fills a definite need.

Of course, the higher the level of position you are seeking, the fewer positions will be open to you. A company may need many engineers but only one vice president of engineering. However, if you contact enough PEs, some will have openings at your level, and in most cases you will have very little competition.

Your Objective in Writing a Personal Sales Letter

Whatever level of responsibility you are seeking, your task is to construct a personal sales letter that generates the greatest number of responses from PEs, including those who are not actively looking for someone. If your letter tries to attract attention by emphasizing what you want, rather than what your PE needs, it will in all probability end up in the wastepaper basket. Your letter should clearly show your reader how you can solve his problem, not just by filling a position but by helping to maximize profits, raise efficiency, lower overhead, increase sales, save on taxes, or whatever else your talents can achieve. If it does, your PE will practically demand to see you for an interview. Wouldn't you in his place?

As you write your personal sales letter, keep in mind that your immediate objective is to get a face-to-face interview. Many job hunters put everything possible in their personal sales letter in the belief that their immediate purpose is to get hired. This is a mistake. You cannot get hired without a face-to-face interview. Your personal sales letter will help you achieve that vital objective. In your letter you must show your PE that what you want is so closely connected with what he wants, and is in his own best interests, that by doing what you suggest he is only furthering his own ends. In short, your sales letter must show that your qualifications are the solution to the PE's problem.

Your Own and Your PE's Needs—How to Satisfy Both

Your needs will be satisfied when you have obtained the superior job that you desire. The PE's needs will be satisfied when he hires a superior executive to fill the open position. You have already taken a giant step toward bringing these two needs together by establishing your professional objective and researching and developing an outstanding resume. In the personal sales letter you are the product; and if you have taken the necessary time to analyze your needs, accomplishments, experiences, and capabilities, you should now know your product very well indeed.

Let's look again at your PE's needs and requirements. If you were a sales manager in a company selling a sophisticated product—say, EDP equipment—what kind of salespeople would you want to hire? What kind of background would you look for? Write down your own ideal job specifications for this position. Mine include a track record of success in selling technical products, experience in the EDP industry, and a technical degree.

How about a senior buyer supervising three other buyers in a medium-size company in the electronics industry? You would probably look for past accomplishment as a buyer in the electronics industry and past success as a supervisor, or as the number-two person in a department of buyers.

Let's try a personnel manager in the insurance industry supervising two other personnel specialists. You would look for someone with a record of success as a personnel manager, successful supervisory experience in the personnel career field, experience in the insurance industry, and a business degree, preferably specializing in personnel.

Notice that the key words in all these examples relate to prior successful experience in the same or a similar function. Naturally, if every requirement cannot be met, the PE will be willing to compromise, provided the primary specifications are met by outstanding accomplishments. Who, for example, would fail to hire a technical salesman who has proved himself by an outstanding record in technical sales, even if he had no degree?

In constructing your personal sales letter, you should strive to meet every possible requirement that a PE would seek. Keep your PE's needs in mind as you develop your sales letter, and present your qualifications so that these needs are filled. This doesn't mean lying or in any way misrepresenting yourself. It does mean emphasizing what you have to offer that is relevant to the job.

The Secret Formula for Writing Your Sales Letter

I have developed a "secret" formula to help you organize your sales letter in a hard-hitting fashion, for maximum impact with your PE. I call it a secret formula because few job hunters use it, or anything like it. Yet it is a simple adaptation of a commercial sales letter in which the unique product you are "selling" is you. Here it is:

Opening/attention getter + explanation + motivation + credibility
+ call to action = superior sales letter

Let's look at each of these items in turn. The opening/attention getter captures your PE's attention, arouses his curiosity, and tempts him to keep reading. The explanation tells your PE why you are writing. Motivation creates a need for your services by describing what you can do for the PE in a persuasive and forceful manner. Credibility convinces your PE that all prior statements in your sales letter are accurate. The call to action tells your PE exactly what to do and suggests that he do it.

How to Write the Opening/Attention Getter

Your opening/attention getter is the lead paragraph in your sales letter. Your objective here is to get your reader's attention and lead into your purpose for writing. To do this, you can employ news, intrigue, shock, or any kind of unusual information, so long as you can relate it to your basic purpose for writing: to obtain an interview. Here are some examples of successful opening/attention getters:

- "I doubled the work output of my department while cutting engineering manhours by 25%. Through lack of control, my department was working on unneeded subsystems. I reduced manhours while doubling productivity on essential work."

This opening/attention getter was written by Tom J., an engineering manager for a large aerospace company. It was so effective that it got Tom interviews for engineering management jobs in both large companies and small, in several different industries.

- "As a professor at the U.S. Military Academy, I taught Juice to Cows who were Goats; 50% of my Goats became Engineers in Juice within 60 days as a direct result of my instruction."

This unusual opening/attention getter was used by Tony B. when he applied for a part-time teaching position at a number of colleges and universities. Tony went on to explain that Juice was slang at the Military Academy for electrical engineering; Cows were college juniors; Goats were cadets with low academic averages; and Engineers were cadets with high academic averages. What Tony was saying was that he taught electrical engineering to juniors with low academic averages, and that 50% of his students achieved high academic averages in electrical engineering as a direct result of his teaching. Few hiring deans could resist reading Tony's sales letter once they had read that opener.

Charlie F., an international commodity salesman, used this opener:

- "I spent 5 years in South America selling American coffee in Brazil and other South American countries."

What an attention getter! That's like selling coconuts to natives of a tropical island. You can bet it materially assisted Charlie in getting interviews for a superior job.

Bob G. was a marketing manager with a small government contractor. Bob's opening/attention getter, which eventually led him to a superior job at a 20% increase in salary, told of a single exploit with that company:

- "I captured a $1.5 million government contract from a giant competitor who had done all prior work. This led my small company into an entirely new business."

If you have been accorded special recognition for some business achievement, here is an opening/attention getter that will fit many different situations:

- "Perhaps only once in a lifetime career as a _____ does a man (or woman) have the opportunity to participate in an event so unique as to warrant special recognition and acclaim. _____ ago I was so fortunate. I was commended for _____."

All good opening/attention getters have one thing in common: they capture the PE's attention at the start and compel him to read on to discover why you are writing to him.

How to Write the Explanation and Why It Is Important

Once you have aroused your PE's interest by your opening, you will raise one major question in his mind: Why is this person writing to me? Your explanation will answer this question and will encourage the PE to read on. Here are some sample explanations for your sales letter:

- "I am writing to you because you may be in need of someone with my training and experience as a marketing manager. If so, you may be interested in some of my other accomplishments."

- "This letter will serve to introduce me and to inquire about your needs for a controller. If you have such a requirement, here are some other things I have done."

- "I am writing to determine if you have a need for someone with my capabilities as a program manager. If you do, you may be interested in additional details of my experience."

- "I am corresponding with you directly in case you need someone with my qualifications as a general manager. Here are some of my other accomplishments."

- "Your company may be in need of a vice president of engineering, and therefore may be interested in additional facts about my expertise in this function."

- "I am writing to alert you to my availability as a business development specialist. Here are some of my other accomplishments in this field."

The explanation paragraph is critical. In addition to telling your PE why you are writing, you will be stating the specific job position you want. Your entire sales letter—from the opening/attention getter to the call to action—must be built around that specific job. As I have mentioned before, many job hunters fail to focus their campaign on a specific job, often because they are afraid of missing out on another job that may be available. As a result, they write something like this: "I am writing in case you need someone with my qualifications for any position that might hold interest for me."

Don't make this mistake. You will seriously weaken your chances of getting a face-to-face interview. Instead of presenting yourself as a uniquely qualified individual with an outstanding background for the PE's immediate needs, you will appear to be a jack-of-all-trades who is easily bettered by almost any competitor in the field. Mention one position and one position only in your sales letter. Concentrate your resources on a single objective. You have only so much space; make every word support the job that you want.

Why does this technique work when the "I can do anything" approach does not? You are aiming your sales letters at that small percentage of PEs who have an immediate need and are thinking of hiring someone in your specialty. Failing to be specific can only weaken your image and dampen the impact of your sales letter. Citing a specific job objective with supporting background and accomplishments will get you high-quality interviews.

Motivation: How to Create a Desire for Your Services

In the motivation section of your sales letter your objective is to create a strong desire for your services. You must make your qualifications so attractive that your PE feels compelled to invite you in for an interview. You will do this by describing outstanding accomplishments, taken from your resume, that support your job objective.

There are two approaches you can take. One is to state what you have accomplished in the function you have decided upon as your objective. Here is an example:

As a missile design engineer, I:
- Patented five separate inventions, all of which reached production.
- Designed more than 140 components of a major guidance subsystem.
- Saved the company more than $5 million in production costs by redesigning a critical gimbal.
- Developed the methodology of computer redesign of old missile components. This saved more than $1 million in design time the first year of operation and is expected to save more than $10 million companywide in three years.
- Authored 7 technical papers published in house and in professional journals. Two were presented at professional society meetings, and one was incorporated into the textbook *Missile Design Handbook*.

The other approach is to list similar functions, all of which support the job you are seeking:

- As director of research and development in a small company, I headed the

R&D division. In 1 year I built funded research and development from 0 to a sustained level of $1 million per year.

- As subsystems manager on a major aircraft project, I was responsible for $50 million in engine subsystems and coordinated the activities of 65 engineers. I prevented a $5 million overrun and a 12-month slippage.
- As program manager of 9 small development programs totaling more than $2 million per year, I was commended by the vice president of engineering for "being on target, on cost, and on schedule while demonstrating exceptional executive ability and decisive leadership."

In developing the motivation part of your sales letter, don't be afraid to use the word *I*. Granted, most successes are team efforts, but would you have been the one pointed at had things turned sour? If so, there is no reason not to state your accomplishments in the first-person singular. A job campaign is definitely not the time for modesty; if you don't tell your PE what you did, no one else will.

Always use short, dynamic, action words such as *directed, led, developed, ran,* and *managed.* A thesaurus will be of assistance in choosing the proper words.

Keep your sentences short and to the point. Write objectively and in a hard-hitting manner, with few adjectives. Let the accomplishments speak for themselves. For example, instead of saying, "I increased sales an incredible 200%," say "I increased sales 200%." Rework your sentences until you get them just right, and check all words for spelling.

Don't cite any accomplishment, no matter how great, unless it supports the job you are seeking. For example, if you are looking for a job in finance and also have an outstanding record in market research, do not describe any of your market research accomplishments unless they relate to finance. Try to state every accomplishment in quantitative terms. Instead of saying, "I gave interviews to a large number of journalists," say, "I gave interviews to 27 journalists." Instead of writing, "I cut cost of sales by a huge percentage," write, "I cut cost of sales by 25%." Don't say, "I prevented a major slippage," say, "I prevented a 4-month slippage."

How to Develop Credibility with Your PE

It is extremely difficult to check on the accomplishments that job hunters claim in their sales letters. Most companies will not release percentage figures, even if known. Nor will they talk about their business in quantitative terms with an executive from another company, especially if that company is a competitor. As a result, many of the accomplishments you have so carefully worked out in quantitative terms cannot be accurately checked. Your PE will recognize this.

How, then, do you establish conviction in the mind of your PE that everything you have said is true? You can do so by stating positive facts about yourself that a PE can check if he desires. You should, for example, state your educational qualifications: "I have a BA in journalism from California State University," or "I have a BS (1962) and MS (1964) in business administration from the University of Wisconsin, specializing in marketing." Or "My BS is in mechanical engineering from the Massachusetts Institute of Technology (1954)." Or "I completed my BA in communications at New York University in 1975."

One question that frequently arises is whether you should state your year of graduation. The answer depends on your situation and the kind of job you are seeking. For example, if you are seeking a chief executive officer's position and you are relatively young, you may want to omit the year of your graduation; if you are older, you may want to include it to emphasize the depth of your experience. Before deciding, consider whether your PE would most likely prefer an older or a younger candidate. Any other information that would document your age should be included only if it is in your best interests.

Whenever possible, tailor your education to the specific job. If you have an MBA specializing in marketing and are seeking a marketing position, state the specialty. If the position is not in marketing, state only that you have an MBA. If you have a BS in industrial engineering specializing in human engineering, do not state your specialty unless the job you are seeking is related to it. The principle, as always, is to insure that every bit of information contained in your sales letter supports your job objective.

What if you haven't graduated from college or haven't attended college? Find something else in your background to use. If you have a professional license of one kind or another—CPA, professional engineer, and so on—use it. If you attended a school but did not graduate, state your educational qualifications in this way: "I attended the University of Minnesota (mechanical engineering)." If you attended more than one school without graduating, you can use this format: "I attended Baltimore City College (business administration), the University of Maryland (business administration), and the University of Pennsylvania (business administration and management)."

If you are not a college graduate but feel you must have a degree in order to obtain a superior job, you might consider enrolling in one of the many nonaccredited institutions across the country. These schools are variously called "universities without walls" or "nontraditional colleges." Some are clearly "diploma mills," though few would admit to being in the last category. They offer nonaccredited degrees based to a varying extent on life experiences. Thus for a fixed sum, which depends on the school, you can become in some cases an almost instant college graduate.

To find out how such institutions operate under the law, I contacted the California Board of Education and discovered that California, like many states, has several classes of college-type institutions. The highest is the one we are all familiar with: an institution that has been accredited by the state. Next on the list is an institution that the state has recommended for accreditation but has not yet accepted. Then comes the lowest class: the state "empowers" the institution to grant degrees but makes no comment on the quality of the education given. At the time of my call, the basic requirement for this legal "empowerment" was incorporation under state laws with $50,000 in educational equipment. Naturally, this figure is subject to change and undoubtedly varies from state to state.

If you are interested in this type of program, check *The Wall Street Journal,* the business section of your local paper, or the Yellow Pages of your phone book. You can also call your state's Board of Education. A number of nonaccredited schools are available to choose from.

I am mentioning these schools primarily because of the relative ease and speed with which they can make you a "college graduate." However, I should also state that in some cases the quality of the education they offer is quite high, and no less an institution than Harvard accepts credit-hour transfers from one of these nonaccredited schools.

How to Call Your PE to Action

The last part of your sales letter is the call to action. You must indicate to your PE exactly what you want him to do—namely, to invite you in for an interview. Here are several variations:

- "I would be happy to discuss further details of my experience in a personal interview."
- "I am prepared to discuss additional facts concerning my background in a face-to-face interview."
- "Please call me after 5:30 any day for a personal interview."

Figures 7 to 10 are sample sales letters for four different job objectives.

What You Should Not Say in Your Sales Letter

As I mentioned previously, and as I will emphasize throughout this book, it is to your advantage not to send a resume to a PE until after the interview. Therefore, do not mention a resume in any context in your sales letter. If you do, at best you will be asked to send it. Then, if your resume is received favorably—and at this point the odds are against it—you will be invited in for an interview. This is not what you are after. You want an immediate interview. You will not attain this objective if you mention a resume.

Never ruin the specialized image you have carefully built in the explanation of your letter by indicating that you are ready to consider some other type of job. If you do, your PE may feel you are in need of a job and will consider anything. PEs like to deal with winners, not desperate job hunters. If the PE volunteers a different type of job and asks about your interest, you can consider that opportunity on its own merits. But it's up to the PE to initiate such a discussion. You must not even hint of the possibility in your sales letter.

Finally, if you are currently unemployed you should recognize that knowledge of your unemployment can devalue your worth with a PE if it is disclosed too early in your campaign. As I will show you in Chapter 11, there are definite advantages of being unemployed in job hunting. However, you should not reveal your unemployment in your sales letter.

Why You Must Include a Telephone Number and Where to Put It

Approximately 75 percent of the requests you receive for interviews will arrive by telephone. Therefore, it is essential to include a telephone number in your sales letter. Don't lose out on a job simply because you cannot be reached. You can have your telephone number printed directly under your address in the sales letter, or you can type it on the page opposite your signature. Either position is fine. Obviously, you should use your home phone if you are currently employed. If you are going to be home only after a certain hour, indicate the hour next to the telephone number. If other members of your family will take the call, make sure you instruct them to get as much information as possible. At a minimum, they should obtain the caller's name, company, and telephone number, even if the caller intends to call back at a more convenient time. You can also use an answering service or a telephone answering device. In your recorded message ask the caller to leave name, company, number, and any other information you wish.

How to Write a Sales Letter to Executive Recruiters

Writing a letter to the "pros" is not much different from writing to PEs. There are executive recruiters and executive recruiters. You will find a discussion of the different types in Chapter 9. For purposes of your sales letter, these differences are not significant. As with writing to PEs, your problem is a statistical one: you must get your letter to that small

---

Figure 7. Sample sales letter of a general manager.

Dear Mr._____ :

As vice president and general manager of a division of a Fortune 500 corporation, I doubled sales from $10 million to $20 million in 5 years.

I am writing to you because you may be in need of someone with my experience and capabilities as general manager of one of your divisions. If this is the case, you may be interested in some of my other accomplishments.

As assistant general manager, I assumed full responsibility for one year during the illness of the general manager. In this period I successfully introduced a new product while increasing profits by 30% over the previous year.

As director of sales, I developed the first comprehensive training program for salesmen. This program assisted in increasing sales by 45% over an 18-month period.

As general manager, I directed the activities of 475 people in production, sales, research and development, engineering, finance, quality control, and personnel. During the five years that I held this position, sales and profits were the highest in the history of this 15-year-old division.

As district sales manager, I increased sales by 500% over a 4-year period through the 11 direct salesmen whom I personally trained.

As assistant to the president of a major corporation, I directed operation studies of four different operating divisions, including analysis of present operations, forecasts, and recommendations. I was commended by the president for "the finest example of profitable staff work I have ever seen."

I have a BS in mechanical engineering from the University of Ohio (1950) and an MBA from New York University (1952).

I look forward to meeting with you in a personal interview.

Sincerely,

---

percentage of executive recruiters who are actively searching for an executive in your specialty.

In writing your sales letter to executive recruiters, use the letter you have developed for PEs, changing only the explanation paragraph. It should read something like this:

- "I am writing to you because you may be currently retained on a search for a senior accountant. If so, you may be interested in some of my other accomplishments."
- "This letter is to inform you of my interest and potential availability for a position as vice president of marketing. Here are some of the other things I have done."
- "I am writing in case you are currently searching for an EDP supervisor of my qualifications. If you have such an assignment, you may be interested in some additional facts about my expertise in this field."

Figure 8. Sample sales letter of a market research analyst.

Dear Mr._____ :

As market research analyst for a well-known market research firm, I directed the largest market research study ever conducted in the dairy industry, involving 42 metropolitan areas in 35 states. This study saved the client over $1 million within 1 year of completion and will ultimately save more than $10 million.

I am writing in case you are in need of a market research analyst in your current operations. Here are some other things I have done:

- Principal analyst. Was principal analyst for more than 50 research studies during a 3-year period. Coordinated the activities of 20 part-time field researchers and 3 junior analysts while doing $300,000 in market research sales.
- Marketing researcher. Participated as staff member of major aerospace company in 5 studies of future weapon systems and competitor capabilities to build similar systems. Was promoted twice in one year for "major accomplishments in assigned responsibilities."
- Publications and presentations. Authored 9 papers published in professional journals of marketing. Two papers were presented at national meetings of the American Marketing Association.

I have a BA specializing in marketing research from Amherst College (1975.)

It would be my pleasure to meet with you to discuss further details of my experience.

Sincerely,

- "I am writing in case you are presently on assignment for a manufacturing manager in the electronics industry. If so, you may be interested in some of my other accomplishments."

At the end of your letter, be sure to say, "Please treat this letter as confidential. My present employer should not be contacted." This is important because a search firm's clients are more impressed if candidates submitted by the firm are currently employed. The executive recruiter is probably not going to contact your employer anyway, but asking him not to emphasizes your status.

Figure 9. Sample sales letter of an accounting manager.

Dear Mr._____:

As controller for a medium-size engineering company, I installed a standard cost system that has saved more than $3 million over a 5-year period.

Your company may need an executive to assume responsibility for the accounting control function. If so, you may be interested in some of my other achievements.

As plant controller, I was responsible for all accounting activities, including financial statement preparation, cash administration, filing of corporate tax returns, and accounting for receivables, payables, and property. Total financial responsibility exceeded $20 million per year.

As assistant divisional controller of a large company, I directed all accounting activities, including statement preparation and product profit/loss analysis. I supervised operation of IBM equipment and developed an advanced budget system that is still (10 years later) in use in this company.

As chief accountant in a small company, I supervised the activities of the accounting department. I developed and installed standard material prices and labor rates, analyzed all contracts for profitability, and developed overhead rates. I was commended by the president for "increasing our finance efficiency by 1,000%."

As consultant-accountant, I performed general audit work for nearly every kind of business enterprise and public and private institution. I installed 12 different systems of financial and cost controls. I progressed from assistant consultant to full consultant in less than 2 years—a first-time accomplishment in this firm.

I have a BA in accounting from the University of Oklahoma.

I would very much like to meet you personally so that we can discuss my background in more detail with a view to my becoming your accounting manager.

Sincerely,

_____

How to Prepare Mailing Lists of PEs

There are many excellent directories you can use to prepare your mailing list of PEs. But two words of caution. Make certain the directory is current; an out-of-date directory is a waste of time and resources and will cut down on the percentage of responses. Use only those directories that provide names as well as companies. You will direct your sales letters not to titles, but to names and titles.

There are directories listing executives in every conceivable industry. Check your library first to see what directories are available. Consult the *Guide to American Directories for Compiling Mailing Lists* and *Principal Business Directories for Building Mailing Lists*. Both volumes list more than

---

Figure 10. Sample sales letter of a public relations manager.

Dear Mr._____:

In ten years of public relations work I have had 225 articles published in industrial magazines, professional journals, and trade papers, resulting in an estimated $2.5 million of publicity for my employers.

My purpose in writing this letter to you is to determine your need for a public relations manager of my capability for your firm. Here are a few of my accomplishments:

- Directed participation in 34 trade shows in 4 industries. Won seven awards for top exhibits.
- Edited 3 internal newspapers with circulations ranging from 1,500 to 55,000.
- Gave more than 100 interviews to journalists and newspeople.
- Developed and directed 44 individual publicity campaigns for different purposes, including new product introduction, entrance into new business, and company image improvement.
- Organized the company visit of 57 groups of dignitaries, including three foreign heads of state.
- Taught 18 courses in writing, public relations, journalism, and publicity in 2 companies and 3 different universities.

I have a BA and MA in journalism, specializing in public relations, from California State College at Fullerton.

If my background interests you, I would be happy to meet with you to give you more details in a personal interview.

Sincerely,

1,000 different directories that can be used as sources for PEs in various industries. The following directories are general in content:

Dun & Bradstreet's *Million Dollar Directory* (executives of 120,000 firms worth more than $500,000, with the top 45,000 firms listed in order of net worth).

Standard & Poor's *Register of Corporations, Directors, and Executives* (400,000 executives of 38,000 companies).

Standard Directory of Advertisers (80,000 executives of 17,000 companies advertising nationally).

Thomas Register of American Manufacturers (100,000 manufacturers by product and location).

Why You Should Mail Your Own Sales Letters

Some firms will offer to mail your sales letter (or resume) to hundreds or thousands of companies at a cost that seems extremely reasonable. For example, one firm advertises that it will put your letters in the hands of 5,000 companies for less than $500. Since the postage alone would cost you more than this amount, it seems like a good buy. Why isn't it? To begin with, these firms cut costs by mailing your sales letter along with those of many other executives. Naturally, this packet of information is sent not to the hiring executive, but to the personnel department. This is not where you want a description of your accomplishments to go. Moreover, even if it went to the hiring executive, it would arrive with the letters of several competitors. It would not go in the highly personalized fashion that is essential for a successful sales letter campaign.

That's not all. Since you did not develop the mailing list, you have no idea where your letter is being sent (size of company, geographical area, and so forth). It could even go to your own firm. And since you have no idea who was on the original mailing list, there is no way you can send a second letter to those executives who did not invite you in for an interview. Finally, this method of scattering your accomplishments tends to lower your overall value, especially if, as sometimes happens, an executive receives more than one copy of your letter. For all these reasons, I urge you to handle your own mailing.

How to Compile a List of Executive Recruiters

Here are some sources for names and executive recruiters:

Consultants and Consulting Organizations Directory, published by Gale Research Company, Book Tower, Detroit, Michigan 48226. Contains information on 5,500 consulting firms, including approximately 500 executive recruiters.

Directory of Executive Recruiters, published by Consultants News, Templeton Road, Fitzwilliam, New Hampshire 03447. Lists 2,300 search firms throughout the United States.

Firms Doing Executive Search, published by the Association of Consulting Management Engineers, Inc., 347 Madison Avenue, New York, New York 10017. Lists approximately 150 firms engaged in search activities.

List of Members, published by the Association of Executive Recruiting Consultants, Inc., 30 Rockefeller Plaza, New York, New York 10020. Lists approximately 60 member firms.

The Executive Employment Guide, published by the American Management Associations, 135 West 50th Street, New York, New York 10020. Updated frequently, it contains information on 129 executive recruiting firms.

One of the best sources for names of executive recruiters is your telephone book. Also, go to your library for phone books covering other cities and states. Don't limit yourself geographically in mailing your sales letters. Even if an executive recruiter works only for a local firm, he will usually recruit candidates from all over the country.

Address your sales letter to Director, XYZ and Associates. If you know a specific recuiter at a firm, use the individual's name. However, the search industry has such a tremendous turnover that, unlike the sources of companies for your sales letters, any directory of names will be obsolete after six months. No matter what source you use, your list of executive recruiters is likely to be only 50 percent accurate.

How to Print Your Sales Letters

You should take great care in printing your sales letter, since it is the only representation of you that the PE or the executive recruiter has until the interview. The letter and envelope should be of high-quality paper, with at least 25 percent rag content. The printing—your address on the letterhead and your name and address on the envelope—should be of equally high quality. You can use either standard-size stationery ($8\frac{1}{2}" \times 11"$) or monarch-size stationery ($7" \times 10\frac{1}{2}"$). I recommend the monarch size because it has been selected by many senior executives across the country for personal use. It will lend a personal tone to your sales letter and will disguise its purpose. Your letter will have a better chance of getting through the executive's secretary and directly into the hands of the hiring executive. The only disadvantage of monarch-size stationery is that you may need to use two sheets, which will increase your costs.

Type your sales letter on the stationery you have selected, using the same typewriter you will use for addressing. Omit the date, the addressee, and the salutation, and don't sign it. Make sure you allow enough space to insert the information during addressing. This master, from which a soft plate for reproduction will be made, must be "camera-ready copy." Take the master to an offset printer. Select the type for your name and address and have this printed separately from the soft plate made from your master. Ask the printer to match the color of ink used for your letter to the color of your typewriter ribbon. When you get your sales letters back from the printer, all you need to do is type in the address and salutation from your mailing list, add the date, and sign each letter.

Alternatively, you can use a word processor or an automatic typewriter, both of which work better but cost more.

The effectiveness of your sales letter will be diminished if the PE's secretary screens it and forwards it to the personnel department. Therefore, on the outside of every envelope type "Private and Confidential." Although this does not guarantee that your letter will not be read by the executive's secretary, the odds are slightly better that it will get through to the hiring executive.

The Results You Can Expect from Sales Letters

Some highly marketable executives who select their target companies extremely well and do everything else right have reported letter-to-interview returns of as high as 50 percent. But such results are extremely rare. Anything in the 3-to-5-percent range is normal, and if you hit 10 percent or better you are doing extremely well. For campaign-planning purposes in this book, I have used 3 percent. This figure will net you 30 interviews on a mailing of 1,000 sales letters. This, along with other methods of generating interviews described in this book, is probably more than adequate for you to obtain a superior job. If your rate is less than 2 percent, you should consider revising your sales letter. Sometimes a minor change or omission of one statement will raise your returns several percentage points. Reread your sales letter several times to see if you can spot what might be turning your PEs off.

Remember, I am talking about actual interviews generated as a result of your sales letters. Replies in themselves count for nothing. If all 1,000 PEs respond to your letters but do not invite you in for an interview, your results are 0 percent. But if you are on target with your material, you can expect 30 to 50 interviews per 1,000 sales letters.

The Types of Responses You Will Receive

Most of the responses you receive from your sales letters will be rejects. Some will come directly from the hiring executive. Others will originate from the personnel department—in which case you may well get a form letter. Such a reply will read along these lines: Mr. Smith, whom you have written, has asked that the writer respond. Though your qualifications are superior, your letter has been circulated throughout the company and there are no openings for someone of your background at the present time. However, because conditions may change, the writer has taken the liberty of placing your letter in the current file and will contact you should any openings arise. Thanks again for considering the XYZ Company.

If you get such a form notice, it may surprise you to learn that Mr. Smith probably has not seen your letter. And it is doubtful that your letter was circulated throughout the company, although your qualifications were probably matched against a list of current requirements on file in the personnel department. I once received a rejection notice from a company that had already extended me a job offer. How is that possible? I wrote two different officers at the company, both of whom might have needed someone with my qualifications. During my interview I learned that the other executive I had written to was out of town. This executive's secretary had intercepted the letter and forwarded it to the employment department. So routine was this action, and the written response, that the employment manager didn't recognize my name, or recall that I had an offer pending with the company.

Another, more insidious type of rejection from the personnel department is the employment application. You will be sent a form to complete so that the PE can better assess your opportunities with the firm. I recommend that you not waste time filling out an employment form unless you are certain that a specific job is available. Otherwise, you risk giving out important information about yourself for no gain at all. For example, even if you don't give your references, it is unwise to list your previous employers at this early stage. The PE may call these companies even if you have no interest in the job. Such premature and needless reference checks can irritate those people who are asked to comment on your past performance. It will definitely break your security if you are conducting a campaign in secret.

What are your possible courses of action? You can treat the employment form as a rejection and write a second sales letter to the PE, following the standard procedure with all rejections. You can contact the individual who sent you the employment application and try to determine if a specific job opening exists. Or you can fill out the employment application without giving references, names of former supervisors, names of former companies, or other information that could compromise your position. For employers, use general descriptions: "a large insurance company," "a major aerospace company," "a well-known consulting firm." For references, use a general title, without the name, address, or phone number: "vice president of a medium-size company," "state senator." Enclose a note stating that complete information will be furnished if there is mutual interest.

Some letters will request additional information or a resume. Try to obtain more information by telephone; then decide whether to comply with the request.

How to Handle Requests for Interviews

Some invitations for interviews are worded so weakly that you may have difficulty recognizing them. Usually they are sent when a PE is afraid of building up your hopes for a job. Such a letter of invitation might read like this: "Though we have no immediate needs for our staff, I would like to talk with you if you have the time. Please call ahead for this appointment." These requests, no matter how weak, should be followed up.

It has been my experience that most requests for interviews come by telephone rather than by mail. This is one reason that it is important for your telephone number to be readily located in your sales letter. Several books I have read on job hunting urge the job hunter to avoid being interviewed over the telephone at all costs. One even suggests that you hang up rather than respond. You will early discover, however, that with the popularity of making appointments by phone, most PEs will do some interviewing in this manner. If the PE is going to pay your travel expenses for the interview, you can bet that he will want to know more than you have written in your sales letter. Therefore, rather than try to avoid the telephone interview, I recommend that you turn it to your advantage by obtaining information from the PE before going in for the interview (See Chapter 7).

Handling yourself on the telephone is an important part of your campaign. If a PE wants to interview you by phone, find out all you can about the job before revealing additional information about yourself. If you do give your PE information, make sure it reinforces your credentials for the job.

Sometimes, a PE will want to talk salary over the phone. It is always to your advantage not to do so until a sale has been made. Use this question to obtain more information: "There are so many factors that bear on compensation that it is almost impossible to give you a figure without knowing more about the job. What can you tell me?"

How Roger G. Used the Telephone to His Advantage

Roger G. was a marketing manager for a small plastics firm in New York City. He wanted to relocate to California. In response to one of Roger's sales letters, the vice president of marketing of a San Francisco company called him. "Before we fly you out here, Roger," he said, "we want to know a little more about you." "Certainly," Roger answered. "What kind of marketing manager are you looking for right now?" Roger managed to ask question after question and took three pages of notes before giving the PE specific information about himself. When he did, he was able to tailor his accomplishments to the PE's needs.

The PE was even more impressed with Roger's potential and set up the interview. But Roger didn't stop there. He went over his notes before the interview, carefully organizing his experiences and background to support his qualifications for this job. Naturally, Roger did well in his interview and received an offer at a considerably higher salary than what he had been earning.

When and How to Write the Second Sales Letter

You should send your second sales letter approximately three weeks after the first. There are several reasons for doing so. Your initial sales letter may not have reached the hiring executive, or business conditions may have changed. An executive can quit, get fired, or be transferred suddenly.

An expansion may require greater manpower needs than anticipated. Budget approvals may come through unexpectedly. Whatever the reason, your second sales letter may be better received than the first. Finally, a second sales letter helps to establish your credibility—that you are "for real." A PE who was on the borderline of responding to your initial sales letter may be convinced by your second letter.

Prepare your second sales letter much like your first, with the following changes: use a different opening/attention getter; write a new explanation paragraph, even though your basic reason for writing is the same; and strengthen your motivators if you did not receive a strong response from your first mailing.

Send your second sales letter to all those PEs who did not invite you for an interview. These include PEs who did not reply at all as well as PEs who sent you a rejection letter, either directly from the hiring executive or from the personnel department. You should also send your second sales letter to additional PEs who have come to your attention since the first mailing. Their names should be on your updated list.

If you are getting good results, you can use your original sales letter with minor changes. However, if your initial mailing brought in poor results, something is wrong with your sales letter (assuming you followed printing and other directions carefully). Reread the early part of this chapter and review the examples. Study every sentence in your sales letter. Sometimes only a small change or omission can make a world of difference. Rewrite your sales letter and send it out again.

How to Keep Records of Your Sales Letter Results

You must keep records of the results of your sales letters so you can determine whether to change your basic sales letter and revise your mailing list for your second letter. You can use your mailing list for your records. To the right of each name draw two columns. Label the first column "Initial Letter" and the second column "Second Letter." As responses come in, put the date in the appropriate column. You can use a code for the type of response: "R" for rejection, "I" for invitation to interview. Always keep all communications and records of communications until your campaign is over.

6

How to Get Interviews Through Answering Advertisements

**The Advantages of Getting Interviews
Through Answering Advertisements**

Ad answering is an outstanding means of generating interviews, second only to your sales letter campaign. A major advantage of answering advertisements is that you can be almost certain that a job is available. In addition, the requirements for the job are usually clearly stated, and there is generally sufficient information to give you an idea of whether the job appeals to you.

The key to beating your competition in answering ads is to make your response exactly what the advertising company has asked for. That is, your experience and qualifications should so clearly meet the requirements listed in the advertisement that your response literally demands an interview.

How to Get Information That Isn't in the Ad

In order to respond effectively, you must know as much about the job as possible. In fact, you shouldn't respond to any advertisement until you have obtained as much information as you can, even from sources other than the advertisement itself. To do this, you must contact two individuals in the company by telephone: the personnel manager and the hiring executive.

If the advertisement is not "blind,"—that is, if the company name is given—one of these two executives may be listed in the ad. If the hiring executive's name is not given, you should have no trouble obtaining it. First figure out the executive's title from the title of the position that is open. For example, if the advertisement is for a marketing manager, the position will probably report to a vice president or a director of marketing. You can then call the company and ask for the name of its vice president of marketing. Use the same technique to obtain the name of the personnel manager—just ask.

What to Say on the Telephone

After you have used the telephone technique explained in Chapter 7 to find out the names of the two executives, ask to speak with the personnel manager. Use the following checklist (or a modification of it to suit your circumstances) to obtain as much information as possible:

What is the exact job title?
Whom does the position report to?
What specific experience are you looking for?
What are the most important functional tasks in the job?
What factors would cause a candidate to be eliminated from consideration for this position?
Is this a new opening? If not, what happened to the previous occupant?
Is a degree required? What kind? An advanced degree? An MBA?
Are there specific problems that you hope the new employee will solve?

Be tactful, friendly, and courteous, but be firm so you can obtain as much information as possible. If the personnel manager tries to put you off by asking you to send a resume, explain that you are highly qualified, but your position is sensitive and you need more information before deciding whether to respond.

Here is one way of starting out after you have gotten through to the personnel manager: "George Smith? Good morning, this is Amy Brown. I heard about your requirement for a financial analyst and I was wondering if I might take a few minutes of your time to discuss the position." Now George Smith is probably reasonably busy. If his ad is any good, he has had quite a few calls, so his initial response may be "It's all in the ad" or "Just send your resume."

It is your job to draw out the personnel manager and get him started on your checklist. Tell him one of the more outstanding tidbits in your background to whet his appetite about your qualifications. Then say you want some information before responding. Or tell him that you currently hold a similar position with a competitor; you know he will respect the confidentiality of your resume, but you would like a few questions answered before sending it.

Another approach is to tell the personnel manager that a friend of yours who works for a competitor claims that the position is not very good. So even though you are qualified and interested in the job, you want to give him a chance to respond to your friend's criticisms before sending off your resume. Use a little imagination. The important thing is to get the personnel manager talking about the job so he will answer your questions.

You may wonder why I have suggested that you call the personnel manager and not the hiring decision manager first. The reason is that the personnel manager is *not* the decision maker. In talking with him first you can afford to make some mistakes, and you will learn a lot more about the job. Then, when you talk with the decision maker, you will appear more knowledgeable about the job.

After getting as much information as you can, thank the personnel manager and revise your checklist for talking with the hiring executive. Do *not* ask the personnel manager if you can talk with the hiring executive. You are under no obligation to announce that you are going to do so. Also, it is much better if you do not, since the personnel manager will resent your infringement and the hiring executive's potential infringement on what he perceives to be his territory.

When talking with the hiring executive, say something like this: "John Wood? Hello. This is Amy Brown. I spoke earlier this morning with George Smith about the financial analyst position opening, and it appears that I am pretty well qualified for the job, but I want to ask a couple of questions if I may." Again, if John Wood asks for a resume, tell him you will send one, but tactfully get him to answer your questions about the job.

When you talk with the hiring executive—who is, after all, your PE— be very careful in your approach, but stay alert to opportunities. Remember, your objective at this point is not to send out a beautiful resume; it is to get a face-to-face interview. A written response may be a required step on the way to the interview, but you may be able to sidestep it by talking directly with the PE. Few if any of your competitors will have gotten this far.

If the PE begins to interview you on the telephone, describe some of your accomplishments that specifically support what you have learned about the job. Ask if you may come in for an interview to discuss your background further. You lose nothing by asking. If you can skip the resume stage, you will save time and improve your chances of getting hired. Also, once you have talked with the PE, you can send a covering letter and a special resume directly to his attention, as well as to the personnel manager.

Do not ask about salary or fringe benefits when speaking with either executive. That is not the purpose of your call, and such questions can cost you both an interview and a job offer.

How to Break "Blind" Ads

In a "blind" advertisement the hiring company hides behind a box number or some other camouflage so that it cannot be identified. Blind ads are often used because a company does not wish to reveal its needs to a customer, because a company wants to conceal an expansion from a competitor, because a headhunter doesn't want his client to know that he locates some candidates through advertising, or because someone is "testing the market"—in which case there isn't any job opening at all. I have even heard of a blind ad being used deliberately as a setup to trap an employee into responding so as to "prove" his disloyalty to an employer.

Blind ads pose a problem for the executive job hunter. Regardless of their intent, they must be "broken" in order to identify the hiring company. If you are currently employed, you must do this without revealing your own identity. One technique that headhunters use to break blind ads is to send a mailgram to the blind address. In the message the respondent explains that he meets every requirement for the position, but because of the sensitivity of his current job he cannot respond fully without knowing the name of the hiring company. This is followed by a brief extract of accomplishments that indicates the high quality of the candidate. The respondent gives an alias (or no name at all) plus a phone number and a request to call. In 50 to 75 percent of the cases advertisers will call the candidate and give him the name of the company.

A typical mailgram for this purpose might look like this:

To: *The Wall Street Journal*
    Box AD-205

Very interested in your advertisement for corporate attorney with petroleum experience. I meet all your stated requirements and have a BS in petroleum engineering as well as an LLB. Have worked as corporate attorney for a petroleum exploration and producing company with $500 million in annual sales. The sensitivity of my present position makes it impossible to respond in more detail without knowing your identity. Please call (717) 555-5996 any day after five o'clock.

You can use either your own telephone number or that of a friend. The advantage of using a friend's number is that it will not be familiar should the blind ad represent your own company. The disadvantage of using a friend's number is that you may not be available to speak with the caller. If a friend takes the call, he should get the company's name as well as the name of the caller, job title, and telephone number. If you take the call, find out all you can about the job and ask for an interview. If the advertiser turns out to be your own company, don't panic. Take the number and use any reason you can think of without identifying yourself to gracefully get off the phone.

Another way of breaking a blind ad is simply to call the newspaper or magazine and ask. Some states require that such information be given out if requested. The worse than can happen is that the newspaper will say no.

If you are conducting a campaign while employed, never respond to a blind ad without checking to make certain the advertiser is not your own company. Many an employee has been discharged for "disloyalty" when he inadvertently responded to a blind advertisement from his own company.

With all the difficulty of responding to blind ads, why bother with them at all? For good reason. Fewer executives respond to blind advertisements than to open ones. Therefore, you will generally have less competition. So do not let the fact that an advertisement is blind deter you from responding. And never underestimate the importance of getting as much information as possible before you answer an advertisement.

How Bob F. Beat Out 300 Competitors for a Job Described in an Ad

Bob F. responded to an ad for an engineer for the Internal Revenue Service. Two weeks later he called to find out what happened. By the sheerest of accidents he spoke with a personnel manager who knew all about the job; because Bob was courteous and tactful, the manager was willing to spend some time talking with him. He told Bob that the IRS had received more than 300 responses to the advertisement and that none of the respondents appeared to be fully qualified. As a result, no decision had been made on interviews.

Bob asked the right questions and discovered exactly what the IRS was seeking. He found out a lot of information that was not in the advertisement. Armed with this knowledge, Bob rewrote his qualifications and accomplishments, tailoring them specifically to the IRS requirements. Within a week after sending out this information, Bob was called in for an interview and was ultimately hired. Of the 300 respondents, he was the only engineer invited in for an interview. He learned later that his first, "I can do everything" resume hadn't even made the semifinals and had been relegated to the "circular file." For Bob, learning everything he could about the job before responding (the second time) made the difference between being offered a superior job and preparing material for the wastepaper basket.

How to Use Response Frequency to Your Advantage

You should know one additional point of importance in answering ads. There is an established response pattern that seems to hold regardless of time of year, geographical location, type of job, or any other factor. Many executive job hunters rush to respond to an ad within a few days after it appears, thinking that it will put them ahead of their competitors. This is a mistake. When a PE has many responses to read, he may not read them carefully. Even a good response can get lost in the shuffle. Also, the hiring executive tends to cut large numbers of resumes or responses rather severely, reducing, say, 200 responses to only 5 for final consideration. A response arriving later will compete only with other later responses and the few "winners" from the huge early response, not the entire 200.

To minimize the chance of your response being overlooked and to take advantage of the reduced competition, do not respond until one week after the ad appears. Don't be afraid to wait. The chances are very slim that you will miss out within two weeks after the ad appears. Most good positions are not filled immediately. Would you want to hire someone for an important job without seeing all the top people available? If you respond too early, you are more likely to lose out than to get an immediate interview and quick hire. Recall that Bob F.'s interview-getting response didn't arrive until almost three weeks after the ad appeared.

How to Draft a Superior Response to Any Advertisement

When you respond to an advertisement, you are aiming at a very small target with a rifle, definitely not a shotgun. Take the advertisement apart line by line and list every requirement you find. Add to this list the requirements you discover in talking with the personnel manager and the hiring executive. For every requirement, list three to five accomplishments from your resume that support your qualifications. Omit a requirement only if you do not meet it.

In your response list the requirements in the same order given in the ad, followed by the requirements you have uncovered on your own. If degree requirements are stated in the ad, give your educational accomplishments immediately after that requirement. If degree requirements are not stated, conclude with this information as you did in your sales letter. Stick to the order in which the requirements are stated in the ad, and follow with the requirements you have ferreted out on your own.

Use and organize the information in your response just as you have done for your sales letter. As with the sales letter, the information comes from the same source: your detailed resume.

Always restate each requirement listed in the advertisement as well as the additional requirements you have identified through other sources. Do this because:

- Frequently when large numbers of resumes are received for one position, a screener looks through them to assure that the basic requirements are met. Restating these requirements clearly makes it easier for the screener, who may know nothing about the job at all, to spot and check off your ability to meet each job requirement.
- Restating each requirement shows that you understand the problem.
- Restating acts as a checklist for you so that you will not inadvertently omit a requirement.

Make your response to the advertisement on the same fine stationery and printing that you have decided to use for your sales letters. You should, of course, keep copies of everything you send out, no matter to whom it is sent.

Why You Shouldn't Respond to a Request for Salary Information

An advertisement may ask you to indicate your salary history and/or desired compensation. It is generally to your advantage not to give out such information until you get to negotiations. At that time you can use it as the situation dictates to negotiate the highest salary possible. Unfortunately, if you fail to give salary information in your response, you may be eliminated from the competition for an interview. If you do list this information, you could be eliminated for being outside the range that the PE is willing to pay. You will also compromise your ability to negotiate for the highest salary possible.

What do you do? You must base your decision on the particular job, your situation, and how strongly the requirement for salary information is stated in the ad. In general, I recommend not giving out salary information, even if requested, until it is to your advantage. Also, as I will explain later in this chapter, if your initial response fails to result in an interview, you will write a follow-up letter. If salary information is requested in the ad, you can include it in the follow-up letter. Do not release it otherwise.

If you have a choice between supplying salary history or desired compensation, it is usually better to give desired compensation, unless your salary history is a strong indication of your outstanding track record. However, if you hope for a sizable increase, it is usually better to hold back. Many industries are reluctant to offer large increases, even if it is to their advantage and you are underpaid.

Now let's examine some sample advertisements and how they should be handled.

Response to an Advertisement for an R&D Manager

SENIOR R&D MANAGER

Highly technical Ohio firm is looking for a senior manager of chemical research. Should have 10 to 15 years of experience managing process and development chemistry in a research lab. Must have strong management background and excellent communications skills. Compensation is commensurate with experience. Outstanding fringe benefits. If you are interested in this position, please submit your resume and salary history in confidence to. . . .

This advertisement has three stated requirements: (1) 10 to 15 years of experience managing process and development chemistry in a researach lab; (2) a strong management background; and (3) excellent communications skills.

Through TTP techniques, let's assume that you have learned the following additional information: the position reports to the vice president of research and development, who feels that good R&D chemists publish. He is proud of the recognition given to members of his division, who received several patents as well as awards from organizations. You have also learned that communication is a major part of the job. In the past top management has been suspicious of research programs. Every program has had to be thoroughly written up and sold through a formal presentation by the senior R&D manager.

The response to this ad should be written exactly like your sales letter, starting with an attention getter and ending with a call to action. Here is a sample letter:

> As product research manager in a rapidly growing company, my success rate for new product development is 57%. This is better than twice the success rate of five other product research managers in my company.
>
> I am writing in response to your advertisement for a senior manager of chemical research. I meet all your stated requirements.
>
> *10 to 15 years of experience managing process and developmental chemistry in a research lab*
>
> In 14 years of managing both process and developmental chemistry, I have:
> - Directed the development of 37 new products and 17 processes that resulted in $250 million in sales potential.
> - Managed development of the "physical fitness pill," judged one of the top 100 inventions of the year 1978 by *Industrial Research Magazine*.
> - Been awarded 17 patents, with 5 patents pending.
>
> *Strong managerial background*
> - Led and directed research organizations ranging from 3 members to multidisciplined groups totaling 27 chemical engineers, research scientists, and medical technicians.
> - Headed the new products division of the Xero Company. Responsible for staffing, planning, budgeting, and scheduling as well as technical output and supervision of 18 chemical engineers, including 7 Ph.D.s.
>
> *Excellent communications skills*
> - Authored 12 papers published in technical journals in 4 countries.
> - Gave 14 technical presentations to such organizations as the American Chemical Society and the International Society of Developmental Chemists.
> - Over a 14-year period, made 71 presentations on results and proposals to customers, potential customers, and top management. Have an 81% rate of proposal acceptance.
>
> I have a BS and MS in chemical engineering from New York University.
>
> I would be happy to discuss futher details of my experience in a personal interview.

Now you are probably thinking that this candidate is uniquely, incredibly, suited to the job. After all, look at the statistics: 57% success rate, $250 million in sales potential, 71 presentations. But stop and think a minute. Have you ever sat down and worked out your own success rate? How many total dollars in sales potential have you been responsible for? If your job requrires presentations, how many have you made during your career? The answers to these questions may surprise you. They represent the kinds of accomplishments you should include in your resume for ready reference.

Response to an Advertisement for an International Attorney

INTERNATIONAL ATTORNEY

New York-based division of a Fortune 500 corporation seeks attorney with 2 to 3 years of major law firm training in corporate and commercial law and litigation to fill important staff position. Duties will span domestic and international operations and will include some travel. Ability to deal at a high negotiatory level, ability to draft sophisticated agreements, and excellent academic and professional records are mandatory. Fluency in Spanish required. Superior opportunity offering immediate responsibility and upward mobility. Generous salary and benefits plan. All replies will be treated as confidential. Forward resume to. . . .

This advertisement has five stated requirements: (1) 2 to 3 years of major law firm training in corporate and commercial law and litigation; (2) an ability to deal at a high negotiatory level; (3) an ability to draft sophisticated agreements; (4) excellent academic and professional records; and (5) fluency in Spanish.

In addition, the ad contains an unstated "requirement" that will greatly assist any candidate in getting an interview. It is implied by the headline of the advertisement and by the second sentence: "Duties will span domestic and international operations and will include some travel." If you have had any international experience, especially in a Spanish-speaking country, you should definitely work it into your response.

Again, through TTP techniques, let's assume you discover that the PE deals primarily in the cosmetics industry. Unless you have cosmetics industry experience, you should not specify the industry in which you worked in your response. Naturally, if you have such experience, you should emphasize it. You have also learned that youth is important. The PE wants someone no older than 30. If you are under 30, you should state your age clearly in your letter.

Here is a sample response:

I was commended by the general manger for "an outstanding job of negotiating and saving the company at least $3 million" when I went to Spain and negotiated a $30 million settlement for my firm.

My letter is in response to your advertisement for an international attorney. I meet all the requirements stated in your advertisement.

2 years of major law firm training in corporate and commerical law and litigation
- In 2 years in a major Chicago law firm, I assisted in handling 13 separate cases involving commercial law and litigation with 8 different corporate clients.

Ability to deal at a high negotiatory level.
- I participated in 10 major negotiations for a major manufacturing company with more than $500 million in annual sales.
- Although only 29 years old, I was chief negotiator for a $30 million settlement with a foreign company headquartered in Spain.

Ability to draft sophisticated agreements
- Drafted 16 separate contractual agreements involving a potential $58 million in royalties and other settlements.
- Drafted a 125-page contract in Spanish.

Excellent academic and professional records
- I have a BA in business administration from the University of Illinois (1973) with an A average.
- I am an honors graduate JDS from the University of Chicago (1977).
- I am a member of the Illinois bar.

Fluency in Spanish
- I am fluent in Spanish—reading, writing, and speaking—and have negotiated in Spanish as well as English.

I would be happy to meet with you at your convenience to discuss my background in detail.

Response to an Advertisement for a Manufacturing Manager

MANUFACTURING MANAGER

We are an expanding Los Angeles-based company in the energy industry. We manufacture a small volume of sophisticated electromechanical hardware for use in our service business and seek the right individual to run our manufacturing department. The manager we are seeking will have 15 to 20 years of manufacturing management experience and should possess under-graduate technical and graduate business degrees. Experience should include responsible positions in materials control, production control, and scheduling, in addition to at least one year of total manufacturing responsibility. Familiarity with electronics and electromechnical applications is essential. Please send resume and salary history to. . . .

This advertisement contains five straightforward requirements: (1) 15 to 20 years of manufacturing management experience: (2) undergraduate technical and graduate business degrees; (3) responsible positions in materials control, production control, and scheduling; (4) at least one year of total manufacturing responsibility; and (5) familiarity with electronics and electromechanical applications.

Also important to the executive job hunter is the information contained in the first three lines: "We manufacture a small volume of sophisticated electromechanical hardware." If you have manufacturing experience with small-volume, sophisticated electromechanical equipment, emphasize this fact. If not, say nothing.

If you do not meet all the requirements, should you still answer the ad? Definitely yes. Many times PEs overstate their requirements because they lack knowledge of the executive manpower available, because they have an idealized view of what it takes to be a success in the job, or because they believe that overstating requirements will get them the best responses. Frequently the individual who is hired does not meet all the stated requirements of the ad. So if you feel you are qualified for a job even though you do not meet every requirement, you should respond. Of course, do not state that you meet all the requirements in your letter (but don't say that you do not meet them either).

Let's say that Hank wants to apply for the job of manufacturing manager described above. Hank graduated with a BS in electrical engineering from the University of Florida in 1964. His first job was as a design engineer in a large aerospace company. After two years he transferred to manufacturing and was put in charge of materials control. He directed a number of projects concerned with low-volume, sophisticated electromechanical hardware. He was promoted twice in the next three years. By 1969 he was deputy electromechanical manufacturing manager.

During this time Hank started going to night school, and by mid-1969 he had finished all his course work except a thesis for his MBA. Then recession struck the aerospace industry, and Hank was laid off. Within a few months Hank was working again, this time as production control manager for a small electronics company making high-volume electronic components. In 1976 Hank was promoted to manufacturing manager. A few years later he realized that for various political reasons he would not be promoted and began looking for a new job.

Now consider Hank's situation. He has almost 20 years of manufacturing management experience, three years in low-volume, sophisticated electromechanical hardware. He has a technical undergraduate degree and has completed his course work for an MBA. Hank has held responsible positions in materials control and production control but has had little direct experience (other than as manufacturing manager) with scheduling. He has two years of total manufacturing responsibility as well as a familiarity with electronics and electromechanical applications. Here is a letter Hank could have written:

> As manufacturing manager for a company manufacturing electronic components, I direct all aspects of production, including materials control, production control, and scheduling. I cut production costs by 15 percent while increasing output by 22 percent.
>
> I am writing in response to your advertisement for a manufacturing manager. Here are some of the highlights of my experience.

15 to 20 years of manufacturing management experience
I have 18 years of manufacturing management experience, ranging from a small company (Advanced Electronic Products Co., Inc.) to a major aerospace company (Douglas Aircraft Company). I have directed the production of small-volume, highly sophisticated electromechanical hardware for electronic actuators, electronic sensing devices, and electronic components.

Undergraduate technical and graduate business degrees
I have a BS in electrical engineering from the University of Florida and all course work completed for an MBA from the University of California.

Responsible positions in materials control, production control, and scheduling
- Responsible for materials control in the manufacture of low-volume, highly sophisticated electromechanical hardware. Saved my company more than $2 million over a three-year period. Promoted twice in three years. Was deputy electromechanical manufacturing manager at age 26.
- Headed production control for a small firm. Reorganized production control department. Developed a sequence of scheduling and manufacturing that saved the company $50,000 per year in manufacturing costs with developed products and $25,000 per year with products developed after the sequence was implemented.
- Promoted to manufacturing manager at age 31 on retirement of former manufacturing manager.

At least one year of total manufacturing responsibility
- Total manufacturing responsibility for 2½ years.
- Responsible for all functions of manufacturing operation, including production control, inventory control, materials control, scheduling, budgets, and costs.
- Cut production costs by 15% while increasing output by 22% and maintaining quality.

Familiarity with electronics and electromechanical application
- 12 years of experience in electronics-related industries.
- 10 years of experience in electromechanical hardware and electronic component manufacturing management.

- 2 years of experience in the design of electromechanical hardware and subsystems.

As I am currently employed as a manufacturing manager, please keep this information confidential. I will, of course, be happy to meet with you to discuss further details of my experience.

Response to an Advertisement for a Vice President

VICE PRESIDENT

This key position, reporting to the president of a major NYSE company based in Denver, demands the skills and intellect of a true professional. The successful candidate should currently be running a successful profit center, hold an MBA from a top-rated university, have a demonstrated fast track record, and be considered highly promotable. Strengths should encompass manufacturing (preferably electromechanical devices) and in-depth knowledge of marketing and cost controls/finance. Chief responsibilities will be monitoring the performance of four of this firm's divisions. Judgment will play an important role in this position, as well as the ability to spot trends and encourage or reverse them. Reply in confidence with resume and salary history to Mr. Jim Bates, International Executive Search Associates.

In this advertisement the executive recruiter has identified himself, so there should be no difficulty obtaining additional information about the job.

Assume that in calling Jim Bates you learn that over the past year two of the four division general managers have been replaced. One of these divisions is still losing money. The average age of the general managers is 43. The president feels that a more experienced executive, preferably with a manufacturing, marketing, or financial background and an MBA, is needed to get things turned around. Currently the president runs all eight of the company's divisions, with three other company officers holding staff positions in production, marketing, and finance. The position of vice president is a new one.

The company is a conglomerate. Four of its divisions are in some facet of the metal-processing industry. These divisions would still be run by the president. The other four divisions are involved in electronics. One division is devoted entirely to electronic defense products; another manufactures various types of alarm systems; the remaining two manufacture small, high-volume electronic equipment. These divisions would be run by the new vice president.

Try your own hand at drafting a reply to this ad. Then go over the following checklist to see if you have covered all the bases.

In completing your response, did you make a list of the requirements in the ad, both stated and implied, and a list of additional requirements obtained in talking with Jim Bates? Your list should include the following:

Stated requirements
Currently running a successful profit center.
Hold an MBA from a top-rated university.
Have a demonstrated fast track record.
Be considered highly promotable.
Strength in manufacturing (preferably electromechanical devices).
In-depth knowledge of marketing and cost controls/finance.
Implied requirements
Ability or past experience in monitoring performance of several divisions.
Ability to spot trends as well as to encourage or reverse them.
Requirements or desirable experience obtained by talking with Jim Bates
Past experience in turning around an unprofitable operation.
Manufacturing, marketing, or financial background.
Older executive.
Experience in the electronics industry, specifically with the Department of Defense, alarm systems, or small, high-volume electronic equipment.

In your response did you open with an attention-getting paragraph and write an explanation paragraph? Did you list each requirement separately, with qualifications and accomplishments supporting each one? Did you quantify your accomplishments in dollars or percentages? Did you close by calling the PE to action?

Why Sales Letters Are Still the Best Way of Getting Interviews

If you have read this chapter carefully and worked the exercise successfully, you have become something of an expert in responding to advertisements. But keep in mind that this technique is limited. Sales letters are still your primary means of getting interviews. You should not answer advertisements and forgo sales letters.

Once your sales letter is written and printed, you can probably send out 300 per day. A 3 percent response—not an unusually high rate—will net you nine interviews per day. Of course, you will be limited by the number of PEs who satisfy your job requirements. But 1,000 sales letters can result in a total of 30 interviews.

In contrast, if you spend all your time answering ads, at most you can handle ten per day; your average will be much lower. To be "on target" with your response, you must spend some time gathering additional intelligence and answering each ad individually. If you generate one interview for every five responses, you will be doing reasonably well. Remember, your competitors for each ad can number in the hundreds. And even if you could answer ten ads per day, you would be limited by the number of ads for the kind of job you are seeking. As a result, you may average only one ad per day or less. So even though the response-to-interview ratio is much higher for advertisements than for sales letters, you are better off concentrating on sales letters first.

With sales letters, you will generate 30 interviews after about two weeks of work. It will take you a full month to get as many interviews by answering advertisements, assuming you can respond to five ads per day with a 20 percent success rate. Finally, it is a fact that only 10 to 15 percent of job openings are advertised. This is one reason why advertised positions are so competitive. They are the most visible and are therefore sought after by the majority of job hunters. The remaining 85 to 90 percent of the openings must be reached by some other means, and your main tool is the personal sales letter.

This does not mean you should not answer advertisements. Ads are an important means of generating interviews, and if you use the techniques outlined in this chapter you will achieve a very respectable success rate. But do not become so enamored of this method that you forget that sales letters are the mainstay of your campaign. Sales letters and other means must be used to reach the unadvertised 85 to 90 percent of job openings.

7

How to Become Expert at Using the Phone to Get Interviews

How to Avoid Getting Interviewed on the Telephone

In general, you should not allow yourself to be interviewed on the telephone. A telephone interview will not result in a job offer and may even cost you a face-to-face interview. However, you will not always be able to avoid telephone interviews. Many PEs will insist on talking to you before setting up a face-to-face interview, especially if they intend to pay transportation and other costs to have you flown to their location.

Since you will have to talk with some PEs on the phone, you should turn the situation around to your advantage. Use the telephone interview to obtain as much information as possible about a job before an interview. Also, as you will soon see, you can use the telephone to generate interviews. How do you obtain information about a job without getting interviewed yourself? You must control the conversation so that you ask the questions and provide only the information you want to—just as in your sales letter—without appearing to do so. Sound tough? Using the Telephone Training Program (TTP), it is not as tough as it sounds.

What the TTP Is and What It Will Do for You

TTP stands for Telephone Training Program. I call it a training program because it not only represents a source of interviews, but also gives you essential training that you need in order to exploit and maximize the number of interviews you can obtain in other ways, to negotiate over the phone, and finally to make the best impression you possibly can before a face-to-face meeting.

The only way to learn to handle yourself over the telephone is to do it. The telephone training program I will outline accomplishes exactly that. You will talk to executives with the authority to hire, and you will present yourself much as you did in the sales letter. Your task is to persuade the executive to invite you in for an interview and to gain as much information about the position as possible. If you become proficient in this technique, you will be able to line up a large number of interviews, as well as significantly increase the number of offers you receive. For the average job hunter, two interviews per day through the TTP is a good number to shoot for.

The TTP should be started as soon as you have your sales letter campaign under way and you have started to repond to advertisements. You should continue the TTP for two to three weeks, or until you have run out of companies in your local area that you might be interested in working for. If you are in a large metropolitan area and an average-size industry, the TTP can probably be continued indefinitely throughout your campaign. You will be honing your telephone manner and getting interviews.

The primary source list of companies for your TTP will be the telephone book. Look under your industry in the Yellow Pages, and simply work down the list. If you do this, you will need to get the executive's name.

Getting the Decision Maker's Name

The quickest and most direct way to get the hiring executive's name is to call the company. Ask the receptionist for the name of the chief buyer, director of sales, or whatever position is directly above the one you are seeking. If the receptionist doesn't give you the executive's first name (the most common response will be "That's Mr. Smith"), ask for it. If you are asked why you want the first name, you can say that you like to get on a first-name basis with people as soon as possible. After you have obtained the executive's full name and written it down, ask to speak to him.

Another way of getting the executive's name is from a trade directory of the industry or from an executive register such as Standard & Poor's. However, trade directories have their disadvantages: they may not contain the name you need; they are very quickly outdated; and unless you are dealing in one industry, you may need more than one.

How to Get Through to the Hiring Executive

The first step in getting through to the hiring executive is to get past the executive's secretary. Many executive job hunters who have no problem getting through a secretary on the job have very real problems breaking through when they are job hunting. The employed executive making a business call doesn't stop to think twice about another executive's secretary and would probably feel insulted if the secretary failed to connect him, even if the other executive was at a higher level. However, the job-seeking executive frequently lacks confidence and feels uncomfortable with the task of calling.

To overcome this feeling, you must maintain a positive mental attitude and practice the techniques for getting through to the executive outlined in this chapter. Before you can get through the executive's secretary you must find out the executive's full name. Then, when you talk with the secretary, you should ask for the executive by first and last name and give your own full name. Speak with confidence (not rudeness or arrogance).

You can also ask your own secretary, if you have one, to call and tell the other secretary that you wish to speak with the executive. This technique makes it relatively easy for you to get through.

Avoiding the Secretary Completely

There is one technique you can use to speak with the executive directly, without talking with the secretary. Do not ask to talk to the executive after you have obtained his name from the receptionist. Instead, call several companies and compile a list of executives' names. Then do your calling after five o'clock. By this hour many secretaries, but not their bosses, have headed for home. Of course, this will not always work. Some executives will be gone after five and some secretaries will still be at work.

Dealing with the Secretary

Once you have the PE's full name, you can use professional techniques to deal with his secretary. Always speak with confidence and say, "Good morning. Jim Jones calling for Bob Smith. Would you connect me please." Give your first and last name and the first and last name of the executive. The only exception to this rule is if you have a title—in which case, use it: "Major Jones (or Dr. Jones) calling for Bob Smith." Do not rush. Concentrate on being smooth but authoritative. If you speak in a natural and confident manner, the secretary will rarely hesitate to connect you with the executive.

You should, however, be prepared in case the secretary questions you further. For example, you may be asked what company you represent. Many executives consult from time to time, and consulting makes an excellent screen when lining up interviews through the TTP. If you have consulted and are asked this question, you can answer truthfully, "The Jim Jones Company." or simply say, "Myself."

You may be asked the subject of the call. One fairly good, but generalized answer is "a confidential business matter." Under no circumstances should you tell the secretary that you are calling about a job. If you do, the secretary will most likely connect you with the personnel department. If you are asked if you know Mr. Smith, you might answer, "No, but I'm looking forward to meeting him."

There are any number of questions that a secretary could ask—and any number of satisfactory answers you can give. The key is to think these answers out ahead of time. Every situation will be different, but your technique will improve as you get experience with the program.

Always be courteous but firm with secretaries, even if they refuse to connect you with their bosses without knowing the full details. In this case, say something like this: "I'm sorry. I fully understand it is your duty to protect your boss from unwanted calls. However, this matter is highly confidential, and I cannot discuss it. Let me leave my name and number so you can let your boss know that I called and he can return my call."

Occasionally, an experienced secretary will suspect that you are a job hunter and suggest that you speak with the personnel manager. Talking to the personnel manager at this point is definitely not in your best interests. So tell the secretary courteously but clearly that you have no reason to talk with anyone but Mr. Smith. And remember, you haven't. Only the hiring executive makes the hiring decision, and it may well be that only he knows of the need for someone in your specialty.

What to Say to the Hiring Executive

Now you finally have the hiring executive on the line. What do you do? Open by saying, "Bob Smith, this is Jim Jones." Then pause and go into the attention getter in your sales letter. Follow the items in your sales letter exactly, stopping only to answer questions if you are asked. However, do not read your sales letter. You will sound too stilted. Make an outline of the sales letter and go over each point in turn: attention getter, explanation, motivation (three to five points), credibility, and call to action.

After your opening, talk on a first-name basis but be respectful. This approach will add a friendly tone to your conversation and will help you maintain your self-confidence. When you have finished the explanation part of your sales letter, pause. Then say, "I am calling because you may need someone with my capabilities as a _____. If so, you may be interested in some of my other accomplishments." Pause again.

At this point the PE will generally indicate his interest or lack of it. Do not try to rush through your presentation in the hopes that the PE will allow you to continue talking. Speak slowly and clearly and give the PE a chance to understand what you are saying. The fact is, even if you give a flawless presentation, only a small percentage of executives will need someone with your background. If you deliver your attention getter and explanation clearly, and if the PE needs an executive with your credentials, he will be eager to hear what you have to say. If the PE expresses no interest (and remember the majority of PEs will not be interested; you are after the small percentage who are), thank him for his time and go on to the next name on your list.

Why You Should Not Send a Resume to PEs

Some PEs will ask you to send a resume. You should avoid doing so if possible. Sending the PE a resume before you have had an opportunity to learn everything you can about the position—and develop a special resume for it—will waste time and could cost you an interview.

There are several ways of handling this. You can tell the PE that your resume is too general or that you cannot send it because of security reasons (you are presently employed). Your dialogue might go something like this: "Frankly, since I am currently employed, I won't send out my resume until there is mutual interest. But I'll be happy to answer any questions now or in a face-to-face interview. Would that be O.K.?" Or you can say that you don't have a resume and then ask, "What specifically would you like to know about me?" You can also handle the problem with a question: "What kind of experience should I have?" As a last line of defense, ask if you can bring your resume with you to the interview. The major advantage here is that the interview can result in a job offer, whereas the resume by itself cannot.

Questions You Must Ask Before the Interview

Asking about the kind of experience you should have is a good technique. You can use it to lead into a number of other questions about the job:

What is the job title?
Whom does the position report to?
What specific experience or accomplishments are you looking for?
What are the most important functional tasks of the job?
Are there any factors that would definitely eliminate a candidate from this position, such as too much experience in a certain area, or not enough?

Do not ask questions about promotion, fringe benefits, or salary. But do probe tactfully for as much information as possible, and take notes while the PE is talking so you can evaluate each requirement against your own background and accomplishments. Then, even if you must send in a resume, you can slant your experience to the PE's needs.

How to Schedule an Interview by Phone

After following the outline of your sales letter completely and telling your PE about yourself, you must make the call to action. If the PE appears interested during your presentation, you can conclude with something like this: "I can tell you are interested in getting together. When would be the best time for me to come in for an interview—on Monday or Wednesday?"

If the PE appears hesitant, see if you can find out why. Sometimes the best way is the most direct—ask. Use the techniques mentioned earlier to avoid sending a general resume, if that is what is holding the PE back. As soon as you have solved the problem, get back to the call to action. Remember, the purpose of the TTP is to obtain an interview. It is your responsibility to guide the PE along this path and show him exactly what you want him to do: invite you in for an interview.

The Limitations of Getting Interviews by Telephone

Although the telephone is a good way of getting interviews, it is not the best way. There are two big limitations to this method. First, as with sales letters, only a very small percentage of the PEs you contact will be looking for someone with your background. It can be very discouraging to make call after call and receive rejection after rejection while you search for that tiny percentage of PEs. Second, telephone calls are expensive. Unless you have access to a WATS line, you will not be able to reach out-of-town PEs by telephone. So the TTP is limited geographically.

Despite these limitations, the TTP is essential to your campaign. If you have integrated the different methods of generating interviews into your campaign plan as recommended, you should always be working on some part of your campaign. The TTP is a means of generating interviews when you are not doing anything else. Also, as with sales letters, you will ferret out jobs that are not advertised.

During the first two weeks of your TTP, when you are spending concentrated time on it, you will generate one to three interviews per day. Equally important, you will learn how to speak with executives on the phone and how to gain and maintain control of your conversations. This is vital for getting interviews that you have initiated through sales letters and responses to advertisements, since most replies will come by telephone. Every day you spend on the TTP will help you sharpen your skills on the telephone. You will be less nervous and more confident about speaking with strangers and persuading them to invite you in for an interview.

Additional Hints for Improving Your Telephone Technique

Whenever you speak with a PE on the telephone, make sure that you listen. If you ask a question, listen for an answer. If you ask a question and the PE struggles for an answer, or there is dead silence, wait. Let the PE answer. Don't jump in to fill the silence and try to help the PE answer the question. The PE is thinking. Give him time. By listening you will learn a great deal. By answering the question for the PE you will learn nothing.

Regardless of your source for companies to call, do not be concerned if you call some of the same executives to whom you have already sent a sales letter. If they have seen your letter and have decided to invite you in, they will say so. If they have decided not to invite you in, you have nothing to lose by calling. What if your sales letter has not arrived by the time you call? If you make a successful presentation by phone, the arrival of your letter will not hurt you. If you did not get an interview by telephone, your sales letter can only increase your chances of getting one.

Always avoid discussions of salary, even if this subject is raised by the PE. You will find advice on how to control salary discussions in Chapter 15. The basic reason for delaying salary negotiations is that the compensation figure you cite may be too high or too low. If it is too high, the PE may eliminate you because he does not intend to pay that much. Yet a PE may offer far more than he intended after he becomes sold on someone during the interview. If the figure cited is too low, the PE may feel that you don't have enough stature for the job. Also, you may find that you wish to raise your salary objectives when you understand more about the job.

Never indicate that you are desperate or anxious for a job, even if you are. If the PE is hesitant about inviting you in for an interview or insists on seeing a resume first, tell him that you would like to save time by bringing the resume in with you. Then explain that you already have an offer and must make a decision within five working days. You would like to meet the PE and see his company, but you don't want to lose a good offer in order to do this. PEs like executives who are in demand and in the running. Make certain that the PE knows other PEs want you.

During your job hunt you will not be able to avoid numerous conversations with PEs by telephone. The TTP will not only get you interviews; it will help you master the art of handling job-hunting situations on the telephone. If you have lost interviews because of your telephone technique in the past, the TTP will insure that you do not have this problem again.

8

How to Advertise Yourself

Why Advertising Yourself the Usual Way May Fail

Pick up any newspaper or trade magazine and you will see numerous advertisements placed by job hunters, usually in the classified section under "Situations Wanted." Despite such widespread advertising, classified ads are not a primary means of obtaining interviews and may not even get you interviews at all. The reason is that few PEs will read your "Situations Wanted" advertisement. Thus you are not reaching the market for your services, and your chances of connecting with a PE who is looking for someone with your qualifications are pretty slim. Also, a good advertisement is expensive and may not be cost-effective compared with other means of securing interviews. Finally, in some media, you may face a one- or two-month delay before the ad appears.

However, advertising can be a useful adjunct to your campaign. To maximize the returns from your ad, you must know where to advertise, what type of advertisement to place, and how to construct your advertisement.

When to Advertise to Reach Your PEs

If you place an advertisement in a general-circulation magazine or newspaper, the only responses you receive may be prospectuses from firms eager to assist you (for a fee) with job-hunting services. In order to advertise effectively, you must select publications that your PEs are likely to read—business papers, trade magazines, professional journals, and so on. Once you have selected the best publications, check to see when your ad will appear so that you can allow for the lead time in your campaign.

What Type of Advertisement to Place

Few PEs take the time to read down a list of classified advertisements on the off-chance that they will find an executive they are seeking. A PE may, however, respond to a well-written advertisement if he sees it. The only way to insure that a PE sees your ad is to use a display advertisement—that is, one that catches his eye because it has been set in a different type size and style than the usual ads. It may have varying space between lines and a lot of white space. It is at least one column wide and at least one inch high. Such an advertisement can cost several hundred dollars or more, depending on the paper or magazine and how many times you run the ad.

How to Construct Your Advertisement

Your advertisement should be an abbreviated version of your sales letter, with the same purpose in mind: to get the interview. The basic parts of your advertisment include the headline, the pitch, credibility, and the call to action plus address.

The Headline

The objective of the headline is to attract the PE's attention and encourage him to keep reading. It serves the same function as the attention getter and the explanation in your sales letter. Your headline should be short and to the point. Make every word count. You are aiming at the PE who has a need for your services and happens to be glancing through the newspaper. If your headline captures his attention, he will read the rest of your ad. Here are some examples of headlines:

"Marketing Executive Available"

"Electronics R&D Manager Will Consider Opportunity"

"Plastics General Manager Seeks New Challenge"

The Pitch

Write your pitch as a shortened version of the motivation part of your sales letter. Rework the statements of accomplishment in your letter, eliminating titles and personal pronouns. Keep the action words and the quantitative descriptions. Your pitch should list no more than five accomplishments. Here are some examples:

- "Developed strategies that boosted sales from $5 million to $10 million in 2 years."
- "Found 7 new markets for 3 old products for $3 million in profit."
- "Turned a loss product into the leading product in 3 months.

Credibility

Use your educational background to insure credibility, just as you did in your sales letter. Again, eliminate personal pronouns and unnecessary words. For example: "BA and MBA specializing in marketing, University of Colorado."

The Call to Action Plus Address

Never omit the call to action when placing an advertisement. Combine your call to action with your address by saying, "Write Box XYZ, *Aviation Week*," or "Call (713) 555-4986." You should list a box number or a telephone number in order to keep your identity confidential until the PE has contacted you. Use a telephone number if possible, since many PEs prefer to respond by phone. Of course, there is nothing wrong with listing a box number as well.

What to Do If You Must Conduct Your Campaign in Secret

If your campaign is to be conducted in secret, you must be very careful in preparing your advertisement. You may have to list a friend's telephone number or use an answering service. To be completely safe, you may not want to list even an area code, since this small clue could give away your identity when combined with other information in your advertisement. State your college degrees but do not give your school or schools. Be careful not to mention any unusual accomplishments or assignments that could allow a business acquaintance to identify you. If you are looking for a superior job in secret, you can advertise, but you must be extremely careful.

Six Effective Ways to Advertise Yourself

In addition to the method described above, there are six ways that are extremely effective for advertising yourself and promoting your expertise in any field or for any job. These are:

Writing articles
Making speeches
Active memberships in organizations
Initiating your own publicity releases
Giving seminars
Presenting papers at professional meetings

All these methods mean direct exposure for you, and exposure means career contacts in two ways. First, it will bring you to the attention of various headhunters who are seeking to fill positions. This is not a short-term thing. However, over the long term, your name will become known. When someone of your qualifications and with your expertise is sought, you are much more likely to be called by headhunters or companies that are seeking to fill top-level positions in your field.

Secondly, the exposure given to you by these six methods means personal contact with people who will see you perform as an expert or will observe what you have done in writing, in public speaking, or in some other way. These contacts can be used by you during your search.

Not only have I seen others use these methods effectively, but I myself have been contacted and offered various positions because of my activity in all six of the above areas. You can do the same thing.

Now, let's look at each method in detail to see how it is used.

Writing Articles

If you have the ability to write, writing articles is an excellent means to obtain publicity, exposure, and eventual job offers. The topic that you select to write about is important. It must be relevant to your work. It could be an opinion about the best way to do things, a special technique or some method you have developed or adopted, or even a survey pertaining to your field. Some journals prefer shorter articles, some more extensive ones. The following books in your library will give you a list of publications that may be interested in publishing an article written by you.

1. *Writer's Market.* Published annually by Writer's Digest Books, 9933 Alliance Road, Cincinnati, Ohio 45242

2. *Directory of Publishing Opportunities in Business, Administration, and Economics.* Published by Cabell Publishing Company, Box 10372, Lamar University Station, Beaumont, Texas 77710

3. *Directory of Publishing Opportunities in Journals and Periodicals.* Published by Marquis Academic Media, Marquis Who's Who, Inc., 200 East Ohio Street, Chicago, Illinois 60611

It is important here that you write for the correct audience. Therefore, you should read very closely the description each publication gives of its readership. You want to write for a group of executives who have the authority to hire you. Therefore, writing for a general or an academic publication usually will be of little help. It is also important that your article be slanted for this readership. Before you begin to write, it would be a good idea to obtain a copy of the magazine that you intend to target.

It is important that the biographical sketch of yourself that you send with your article identifies the company that you are currently working for. It should also include other items in your background that will establish your expertise for writing the article. Remember, these things may interest PEs as well.

Making Speeches

Making speeches in your area of expertise is an excellent way of becoming well known as an expert in your industry and as a potential high-powered executive for any company. It is also a very easy way to publicize yourself, since there are many more organizations that need speakers for their luncheon, supper, or other meetings than there are speakers available to do the job. If you line yourself up for only one speech a week, and even if the group you address numbers only 20 people, in a year you will have made over 1,000 contacts who will recognize you as an expert in your field.

What subject should you speak on? Choose a subject that can demonstrate your expertise and that will interest as large a group as possible. For example, if you are an accountant and have some expertise on a certain aspect of corporate accounting such as corporate tax laws or how to accomplish zero-base budgeting, this may be a good area to speak on. If you are an engineer and have knowledge about design engineering, quality control, or some other technical area, this too may be of great interest to various groups.

Speeches may vary in length from 15 minutes to as long as an hour. Prepare the outline of a presentation that will allow you to go either way. You can then either shorten or lengthen your speech according to the occasion. This way, you can address many more organizations than you could if you simply had a single speech of a set length.

Your next step is to find organizations that would like to have you speak. As I mentioned previously, many organizations have monthly meetings and are eager to invite speakers on subjects that will interest their membership. One way of locating such organizations is simply to use the Yellow Pages of your telephone book and look under "Associations." Call every single association listed. Tell them all that you are an expert in your particular area and that you would be willing to give them a free presentation on this subject. If they ask how long the presentation would be, tell them you would be happy to tailor it from 15 minutes to an hour depending on their needs. They will then tell you exactly what their needs are. Be sure to think of some highlights to mention on the telephone that not only show that you know what you're talking about but also demonstrate that the subject would be of interest to your prospective audience.

You may also find prospective groups to speak to by calling up major companies and asking whether they have a manager's club. If they do, the club will have a president, a secretary, or someone in charge of entertainment. Many major companies have management clubs, and as many as several hundred or more people may attend each event. What a great way to make contacts who may turn out to be prospective employers later on down the line!

A third way to make contact for speeches is to go to your library and look at a book called *Encyclopedia of Associations*. This lists every major association in the United States. You can write a short letter to those that are not in your local area, telling them about your speech and the fact that you are offering to make such a speech to their organization. A short, direct mail sales letter like those used for finding a job can easily bring you a number of different engagements.

As with writing articles, a fringe benefit of making speeches is that in many cases you will be paid for your presentation.

Active Memberships in Organizations

Being an active member in a number of organizations is another great way to gain exposure for career contacts. However, active membership means exactly that. It means you cannot just join an organization but should go to its functions and, if possible, become an officer. These organizations may be professional—such as the American Marketing Association, which has local chapters all over the country. They could be related to the college or univeristy from which you graduated, or they could even be social organizations of one type or another. All these are outstanding opportunities to make contacts. Even in an athletic club it would be unusual not to make friends and to know who is doing what. If you have the opportunity to become an officer in the organization, you can then demonstrate your leadership and executive management skills. Whenever you may need a new position in the future, you have the contacts ready and waiting who are already aware of your abilities.

Initiating Your Own Publicity Releases

Every major firm and a number of knowledgeable smaller firms give publicity releases to newspapers, interested magazines, and other publications whenever they can. This publicity usually results in additional business for them.

In the same way, you can initiate your own publicity releases for whenever you do something. This will demonstrate your ability, make you look good to your present boss, and also get you noticed by others in your field, who may then regard you as an expert. Now, you may be thinking, how can I give a publicity release on anything if I am working for a company that handles publicity itself? Most companies have a publicity department or at least someone handling this task. You may be able to persuade your company's publicity department to do an occasional release. But remember, the company's purpose is different from yours. The company's objective is to publicize the company, not to provide the personal publicity you are going to use to help you get a superior job. Therefore, you shouldn't depend on your company's publicity department entirely, but should send out your own releases whenever something happens to you or you have something to say that (1) demonstates expertise and (2) may be of interest to someone and would therefore be published by a newspaper, magazine, or journal of your industry.

What might the topics of such publicity releases be? Well, for one thing, if you succeeded in publishing an article or giving a speech, you might want to publicize something you said or wrote about if it is of interest to other people in your industry. You can then indicate that this was said during such and such a speech or in such and such an article. This publicity will expand your opportunities for additional speeches and articles, as well as expose you to opportunities for a superior job. If you are doing something outside of work which has nothing to do with your current job but which is in the same field, publicity here will help you also. Perhaps you are an engineer and have designed something outside of work that does not interest your own company. A publicity release under these circumstances is perfectly legitimate, and it will gain publicity not only for your invention but also for your expertise—while not offending the company that you are currently working for.

Writing a publicity release is not difficult. You simply write at the top

"For Immediate Release" and then go on to describe whatever it is that has happened that you wish to have publicity on. If you have a photograph of yourself to include with the release, this can sometimes be printed as well and will definitely help to publicize you and make more people read the release.

If you wish, you may use a cover letter with the publicity release, addressed to the editor of the magazine or newspaper, or the editor of the department in which you are seeking publicity. However, this isn't strictly necessary. A publicity release by itself can be extremely effective as a single enclosure.

How do you know where to send your publicity release? One excellent source is *Standard Rate and Data Service* (or *SRDS*), which publishes a number of different directories periodically and can be found in your library. These include directories of business magazines, consumer magazines, and newspapers. There are literally thousands of publications available, so, again, you must seek your target market and send the publicity release only to those that serve your target audience of PEs who may be interested in hiring you at some time in the future.

Giving Seminars

Sharing your expertise with others through seminars is an excellent way of promoting yourself, becoming well known, and gaining the exposure that will lead to outstanding career contacts. There are several ways of doing this.

One is setting up your own seminar, writing all the promotional material yourself, and paying for the printing, the rental of mailing lists, and other expenses—that is, doing the entire project as an entrepreneur. Many individuals do this full time and earn substantial financial rewards for their efforts. A thousand dollars or more per day is not unusual. In fact, one very well-known seminar company started in exactly this fashion, with a government employee using his annual two-week vacation to give seminars on government contracting. Eventually he left government employment to do this on his own, year round, and today this same company has trained thousands of people in industry interested in doing business with the government. However, doing everything as an entrepreneur requires a great deal of effort, and if your primary purpose is to seek career contacts for finding a superior job, it is not the most efficient way of getting this accomplished.

There are alternative ways that are much easier. One is to go to local universities and colleges in your area and contact their continuing education department. Almost every college and university in the United States today has a program of educating executives through various seminars. In some cases, these seminars are taught by faculty from the university. Many, many others are taught by business executives like you who have expertise in some area of industry, including marketing, engineering, economics, and legal issues.

A third way to start giving seminars is to contact organizations that specifically give seminars to executives. One example of this is the American Management Associations, which conducts seminars and courses all over the country on a continuing basis. Write to American Management Associations, 135 West 50th Street, New York, New York 10020, and ask for the current course catalog. From this catalog you will see various types of courses that are available. You may then contact the person in charge of the specific functional area you are interested in and volunteer to give a course in the area noted.

Presenting Papers at Professional Meetings

Mere attendance at professional meetings is a good thing for your career, since it in itself is a method of exposure and contact with other executives who may have the power to give you the superior position that you seek. However, a far better way is to present a paper at such a meeting, since, again, this establishes your expertise and also exposes you to many more people through your presentation than you would meet in the normal course of events at a conference or professional meeting. Once more, this is both a long-range and a short-range proposition. In many cases you can actually meet contacts immediately interested in hiring you for various positions. For the long range, many executive recruiters use conference papers and lists of attendees as sources for potential candidates for positions they are seeking to fill.

In summary, advertising yourself should be only an adjunct to your main campaign. But such a campaign can be an effective adjunct if you follow the following advice:

1. If you are going to advertise in media, advertise in media that your PEs are likely to read.
2. Make your ad a display ad, in effect, a mini sales letter.
3. Construct your ad in four parts: headline, pitch, credibility, and call to action combined with address.
4. List the telephone number and/or a box number.
5. Prepare for your search for a superior job by using all six long-term means of advertising: writing articles, making speeches, active memberships in organizations, initiating your own publicity releases, giving seminars, and presenting papers at professional meetings.

9

How to Get a Job Through a Corporate Headhunter

The Difference Between Employment Agencies and Search Firms

There are two distinctly different breeds of corporate headhunter: the employment agency and the search firm or executive recruiting firm. The differences between these two varieties have blurred in recent years. However, many agencies and search firms still perceive their functions to be different, and in some cases the differences are real and will affect your actions. It is important to understand these distinctions between types of headhunters and to identify the type of firm you are dealing with, regardless of what name it goes by.

Once upon a time, employment agencies represented only the interests of the job hunter, known in agency jargon as the "applicant." The applicant "registered" with the employment agency, which in turn kept master files of applicants in every functional specialty. A potential hiring company contacted the employment agency and described the attributes it sought in a new employee. The agency consulted its extensive files and immediately produced a number of indivduals meeting the basic criteria. These individuals (in some cases half a dozen or more) were contacted and sent out to interview for the job. A successful applicant—one who was hired—paid a certain percentage of his annual salary to the employment agency. Usually the jobs filled by the agency were not senior positions, and the responsibility for screening the applicants and checking references was left to the hiring company.

In contrast, executive recruiting firms, which grew out of management consulting, worked only for the hiring company. The client engaged the firm in a "search assignment," providing it with a detailed description of what it desired in a new employee. This description, known as the job specification, included such information as exact school attended, height, weight, personality, and spouse's personality. The potential employee was not an applicant, but a "candidate."

The search firm frequently helped to develop job specifications and spent considerable time with the hiring company starting the search. Generally, an executive recruiting company searched only for senior people and received a retainer on starting a new assignment. The search firm received partial payment even if the search was not successful. Final payment was made only after at least one of several candidates was recruited, screened by the search firm (including reference checks), sent for an interview, and hired. The total fee to the hiring company ranged from 25 to 30 percent of annual salary.

The search firm claimed to differ from the employment agency in that it worked for the hiring company rather than the job hunter. In addition, the firm generally recruited only senior executives and was paid whether or not it filled the position. Unlike the agency, the search firm actively screened its candidates thoroughly, provided reference checks, and offered a money-back guarantee on its placements.

Today, in many cases, the differences between these two types of companies are inconsequential and difficult to distinguish. Most employment agencies will accept job orders where they are paid by the hiring company; indeed, some agencies handle only fee-paid positions. Today many agencies fill top management positions, including vice presidents, presidents, and chief executive officers. At the same time, many respectable search firms now accept assignments for lower-level positions as well as higher-level ones.

Much the same has happened to methods of payment. I know of employment agencies that work on a retainer basis. I also know of search firms that accept assignments for which they are paid only for a hire, or have a subsidiary that will. Recruiting versus files of resumes? Many search firms maintain comprehensive files, and many employment agencies go out and recruit. Screening and reference checks? Both types of firms do reference checks today. Generally, however, a company that is paid a retainer does a more thorough job of screening and preinterviewing. And yes, you guessed it, most employment agencies offer a money-back guarantee to the employer as well.

In many states the difference between a search firm and an agency is defined by law according to the level of annual compensation paid to the candidate placed. In California, for example, a firm that places individuals earning less than $20,000 per year is licensed by the state as an agency regardless of its operating policies. A firm that limits its business to individuals earning more than $20,000 is not required to become licensed as an agency.

Unfortunately, this definition often fails in practice. Many agencies place executives who earn more than $20,000 per year; in fact, such executives may comprise most of their business. Similarly, many firms meeting every other definition of a search firm will maintain an agency license, have a wholly owned agency subsidiary, or ignore the law. As the president of a leading search firm told me: "When you have just success-fully placed your third $65,000-a-year executive with the same company and the pleased CEO, as he hands you a good-size check for your services, looks you in the eye and says 'Wonderful job, now find me two junior assistant accountants,' you do not say no."

If the differences between agencies and search firms are not great, why not treat them the same? First of all, how the firm perceives itself will govern how you use it to your advantage after initial contact. Second, in some cases the differences are significant. Some firms deal only in executives making $50,000 or more. And some firms are totally unprofessional, even unethical, and are better left alone.

Even an expert can have difficulty distinguishing between an agency and a search firm by company, and new firms in the industry are founded every day. Therefore, as described in Chapter 5, in writing sales letters to executive recruiters and developing your mailing list, treat both types of headhunters the same. After you have made direct contact, vary your techniques according to the firm's philosophy and modus operandi, as discussed below.

What Headhunters Are Looking For and Why

In general, search firms will not be interested in job candidates unless they are currently employed. Most agencies are not concerned with employment status and may even prefer unemployed job hunters, since they feel such candidates are easier to control and will accept a position more readily. This is part of a complex formula that some firms use to determine the greatest probability of filling a position. The formula involves a candidate's willingness to accept a position weighed against his marketability, or what the headhunter perceives to be his strengths and weaknesses. Remember, an agency headhunter usually doesn't get paid unless a candidate is hired. Thus the agency may weight a job hunter's willingness to accept an offer heavier than his marketability to a PE. A search firm, by contrast, usually gets paid whether or not a candidate accepts a position and is in a monopoly position regarding a given search assignment. Such a firm will usually consider marketability more important. Therefore, if you have established a consultancy to mask your unemployment, you should retain this mask in dealing with a search firm and consider dropping it in dealing with an agency (after you have had a face-to-face interview with the agency headhunter to assess the situation).

When and How to Deal with an Employment Agency

Although many agencies place highly paid executives, they usually prefer to work with candidates making less than $40,000 a year. The faster agency headhunters can move their human merchandise (after all, that's why they're called headhunters), the more money they will make. If they spend too much time with one difficult-to-place candidate or one difficult job order, they will lose money. Statistically, if you're making less than $40,000 a year, you will be easier to place than if you are making $40,000 a year or more. If you fall into this easier-to-place category, it is in your interest to work with agency headhunters. Spend some time with four or five good agencies in your area.

Agencies vary greatly in the training given their employees, the contacts they have, and how much they can do for you as an executive job hunter. Even within a single agency, the capabilities of individual headhunters will vary. Therefore, it is important to check out an agency and its employees thoroughly. An inept headhunter not only will waste your time but may make serious mistakes that hurt your campaign.

You can check out an agency by calling your local Better Business Bureau and asking if any complaints have been registered against the agency. You can also ask friends and members of professional organizations to recommend agencies in your area. Finally, you can simply call the agency and speak with the specialist in your functional area or industry. Ask how the specialist works and get an idea about his honesty and representation of your interests to the agency's clients.

Why You Shouldn't Reveal Your References Immediately

Most of the agencies and search firms you contact will ask for references. Again, you should not reveal references until mutual interest with a PE has been established. Even someone you consider a solid reference will be bothered by repeated calls. Explain to the headhunter that you have excellent senior references and are willing to make them available. However, you do not want your references bothered until you and your PE have expressed interest in each other. This will guard against your references becoming lukewarm by the time you really need them.

Headhunters are likely to be more insistent than PEs about receiving references immediately. Do what you can to withstand the pressure. Many headhunters will respect your wishes. If they insist on the information before proceeding, try to find out if a definite position exists. Get the headhunter's assurance that your references won't be called until you agree. If you have any doubt about working with a headhunter, don't give out your references.

How to Handle Salary Questions from Headhunters

Agencies and search firms will probably request your salary history or at least your current salary. Unless your qualifications are so outstanding that you have no worries about getting a job offer, you will probably have to reveal this information. In most cases, the headhunter will jot down a figure 15 to 20 percent higher than your current earnings as your maximum asking salary.

You may be able to get around this problem by telling the headhunter that you consider your current or previous salary confidential, but that you are prepared to consider a position at a salary of $X. Such an approach is perfectly effective if you are currently underpaid. Most headhunters will accept your asking figure, provided it is not out of line with your responsibility, industry, and other factors related to the job. You can also state your salary in terms of the total compensation you receive. That is, include retirement plans, bonus, and other fringe benefits. Finally, you can include an expected raise in your salary figure. Remember, whenever possible, you should avoid revealing your salary to the headhunter. If you must, give the highest figure you can, consistent with what is paid for the services you are prepared to perform in your industry.

How to Handle an Interview with an Agency

There is a crucial piece of information about headhunters that most executive job hunters overlook. You must find out whether the headhunter intends to work with you. Remember that many headhunters are paid only on a contingency basis. They do not have time to see most candidates more than briefly and to put their resumes on file. It is your job to convince the headhunter that you are a highly marketable commodity with a high probability of placement. Find out if the headhunter considers you in this category. Some headhunters will come right out and say that you have little chance of being placed with their clients. Do not be discouraged by this information: remember, the headhunter's criteria for placement are not the same as yours. But don't waste more time with a headhunter if you come up against a dead end. If the headhunter does not volunteer the information, ask him directly about your chances of being placed.

Obviously, it is in your interest to convince the headhunter that you have a good chance of getting an offer from one of his clients. Read Chapter 15 on interviewing before you talk with the agency. The same techniques you use with a PE are applicable here. If you are successful in convincing the headhunter that you can be placed rapidly, he will line up interviews for you. If not, your resume will be buried in a file and you may never hear from the headhunter again.

To succeed in an agency interview, you must impress the headhunter with your interviewing ability. Let the interviewer know that you are eager to find a job and are prepared to act quickly to accept the right position. Do not volunteer the information that you are working with other agencies or that you are conducting your own job campaign.

If you are asked how long it will take you to move from your present job to a new one, do not give an excessively long period. Three weeks is about maximum. If you are asked where you think you will be six months from now, the only acceptable answer—if you are serious and confident about getting a new job—is in your new job.

If the interview does not go well and the interviewer seems uninterested, find out why. In general, headhunters are less reluctant than PEs to tell you what's wrong. Therefore, ask the interviewer directly: "You seem to feel that I do not have much chance of getting an offer from one of your clients. Can you tell me why you feel this way?"

What You Should Not Do When Dealing with Agencies

Do not let any agency scatter your resume over the countryside, sending it to "hundreds of companies." Although this may seem like a great idea, it can hurt your job campaign. Widespread distribution of your resume will work against your precise, on-target sales letter campaign by providing PEs with general rather than specific information about you. The information could even appear to be conflicting. Further, an unsolicited resume from an employment agency can devalue your worth to PEs. Many a well-qualified candidate sent out by a headhunter has been rejected by a client because the client had received resumes on the candidate from several different agencies.

If you are currently employed, it is obviously dangerous to let an agency send your resume to firms you do not know. (If you are conducting a campaign in secret, read the next chapter before proceeding.) Finally, remember that you are conducting your own job campaign. Even though you use headhunters as part of this effort, you must retain control over the situation. You should have final say on what firms are contacted in your behalf.

Some agencies will ask you to provide a list of companies that you have already contacted. I recommend that you do so only if you have already interviewed with a company and did not receive a job offer. Some unscrupulous headhunters will, without your knowledge or permission, use such a list to solicit job orders; they may even submit other candidates to companies that you are negotiating with. For this reason, you should give the headhunter only the names of companies you are no longer interested in. Also, do not tell the headhunter that you are currently negotiating with any company. Generally, if you have contacted or are contacting PEs on your own, you will not be attractive to the agency headhunter, who gets paid only if *he* places you.

What to Do When You Are Called by a Headhunter

You may not even be thinking about a new position when one bright and sunny day you are called by a headhunter who attempts to recruit you or seeks your help in finding someone else. What do you do?

Even if you are secure in your job and uninterested, you never know what the future will hold, so do not be abusive, no matter how inconvenient the call or how bad a day you are having. The headhunter may have some truly lucrative opportunities. Even if you aren't interested, you may be able to help out a friend, and you will be making a valuable contact for the future. Be aware, too, that the headhunter may be using the indirect approach. Even if he asks for recommendations, you may be a potential candidate yourself.

Let the headhunter give you as much information as he wants, but don't reveal information about yourself during this first conversation. Ask the headhunter to call you at home, and set a definite time for him to do so. It is much safer—and fairer to your employer—to discuss a job opportunity from your home. You will have time to organize yourself and decide if you are interested in the position.

When you receive the headhunter's call, your primary objectives are to learn all you can about the job (using the techniques described in Chapter 7) and to find out where the headhunter got your name. There are many sources of your name other than recommendations. The headhunter may even be shooting in the dark, knowing only your name and function. If this is the case, you may have to go through a lengthy qualifying process before being interviewed for a job.

In this telephone interview you should appear neither overly coy nor overly eager. Tell the headhunter that you are doing extremely well in your present position but would be prepared to consider a superior career opportunity. Keep your dignity. Do not "spill your guts" about anything, and make certain that a superior opportunity exists before giving out extensive information about yourself.

If you are not interested in the position, say so and say why. If you know some friends who may be interested, it cannot hurt you to recommend them. Describe a few of your outstanding accomplishments and the kind of job that would appeal to you. But do not send the headhunter a resume or any other information unless you are thinking about leaving your present job and unless a specific opportunity exists.

If you are interested in the position, make certain that the experience and accomplishments you describe fill the requirements. Ask intelligent questions about the job. Use techniques outlined elsewhere in this book for interviews and other steps in the hiring process.

Headhunters do make executive placements, lots of them, or they wouldn't be in business. However, it is a mistake to see a couple of headhunters, then sit back and wait for results. Use headhunters to your advantage in getting a superior job, but remember that they are only one part of your job campaign. They should *not* be considered the most important part.

10

How to Find
a Superior Job
in Secret

The Advantages and Disadvantages of Being Employed
While Job Hunting

As a rule, it is better to look for a new job while you are still employed in your old one. Being employed while job hunting has definite advantages. You are under no time pressure or financial pressure, and you are generally more attractive to a PE than an unemployed candidate.

The main disadvantage of job hunting while employed is the need to conduct your campaign in secret. If your present employer finds out that you are looking, you can lose any chance for a promotion or raise—and you may even be fired. Unfortunately, the secrecy requirement makes it difficult or impossible to use some of the techniques discussed in this book. It will also lengthen your job campaign.

The basic principles outlined in this book will help any job hunter find a superior job. This chapter will focus on the changes you must make if you are employed to conduct your campaign in secret. The techniques described will increase your security at your present job and help you to perform your duties adequately while job hunting.

How to Reorient Your Sales Letter Campaign

Depending on your job level and other factors, it may not be wise to distribute sales letters through your industry, since your present employer could learn of your campaign. To get around this problem, you can use the third-party technique. Write your sales letter so that it appears to describe someone else, not you. For example, in your attention getter do not say, "I turned a $500,000 loss situation into a profit within six months." Instead say, "I know an executive who turned a $500,000 loss situation into a profit within six months." For your explanation paragraph say something like this: "If you need a general manager, you may be interested in some of this executive's other accomplishments."

In the motivation part of your letter, describe your accomplishments just as you would in a sales letter. Change the credibility paragraph to read something like this: "This executive has a BS in engineering from Iowa State University and an MBA specializing in finance from the University of Illinois." In the call to action say, "If you would like further details, call or write the undersigned, who will arrange a personal interview."

What to Do When You Are Contacted by the PE

When you are contacted by the PE, reveal yourself as the job candidate only after the PE is committed to an interview. If you have any doubts about the authenticity of the call, don't reveal yourself until the interview or until you have enough time to investigate the company.

Obviously, this method is hardly foolproof; and if your present employer gets hold of your sales letter, it will be obvious just who you are fronting for. However, the third-party approach does allow for an element of doubt and makes it more difficult for your present employer to take punitive action against you. It also has the advantage of being more objective than a first-person letter, since it appears that someone else is commending you rather than you saying good things about yourself.

Who Should Sign Your Third-Party Sales Letter?

Depending on your situation and the resources available to you, you may not want to sign a third-party sales letter yourself. You can increase security by having a friend act as your front. Your friend would sign the sales letter, take telephone calls, and set up interviews for you. If you use this method, you need not admit deception, as you must eventually do if you sign the letter yourself. Also, there is less chance that your employer will find out about your job campaign. Naturally, if whoever signs the letter is someone well known or important, such as a company officer, this will increase your response rate.

Brief whoever signs your letter on exactly what to say on the phone and what questions to ask the PE. Naturally, you want to get as much information as possible so that you can decide whether to call the PE.

If your campaign is to be conducted in secret, use the third-party sales letter in writing to headhunters. After a headhunter calls you, reveal your identity only if the recruiter and his modus operandi sound right. If the executive recruiter has no specific assignment for you, make certain he understands that you do not want any information on your background distributed to his clients.

Most executive recruiters are ethical. They realize the extreme confidentiality of the information you give them and will not release any information that could get back to your present employer. However, it is wise to stress to any headhunter that you are presently employed and that the information you provide is sensitive. Remember also that there are all kinds of headhunters, so you must be cautious.

How to Respond to a "Blind" Advertisement

One of the most difficult tasks in a secret job campaign is answering a "blind" ad. Responding executives are often horrified to discover that what appeared to be a truly outstanding opportunity was a job at their level or lower in their own company. Imaginative personnel managers can do wonders with the most prosaic of jobs. Executives who blissfully respond with little caution or forethought are needlessly risking their present jobs.

You should respond to blind ads that hold interest for you. As mentioned previously, blind ads usually generate fewer total responses than open ads, since many employed job hunters are reluctant to use them. Thus a significant portion of your competition is eliminated before you even pick up your pen.

Before responding to the blind ad, you must discover who is behind it without revealing your own identity. Some methods of concealing your identity while breaking a blind advertisement have been discussed in Chapter 6.

Another technique you can use is the third-party approach. As in the third-party sales letter, begin your response with "I have a friend who . . ." or "I know an executive who. . . ." Then lead into a special explanation: "I am writing to you in response to your advertisement for an advertising manager. However, because this executive is currently employed, he does not wish to reveal his identity until your identity has been established."

Take the advertisement apart as discussed in Chapter 6, listing each requirement and describing specific accomplishments that qualify you for the job. Your concluding paragraph should read along these lines: "This executive will be happy to meet with you to discuss further details of his background and the position. Please contact me at the address or phone number listed in this letter."

Another way to discover the advertiser's identity is to use an answering service at a rented address. In this case, you should write a first-person response to the advertisement, ending with the following sentence: "Because of the sensitivity of my current position, I cannot reveal my identity at this time. Please call or write the answering service listed in this letter." Don't forget to instruct the answering service not to reveal your name to callers.

Finally, you can rent a box number and use that for your address, signing the letter with the box number rather than your name. At the end of the letter explain why you are not revealing your identity and when you will be prepared to do so. The major disadvantage of this method is that it requires the PE to respond in writing. Many PE's prefer to contact prospective employees by telephone. Keep in mind that any method that does not allow a PE to call will cost you a certain number of interviews.

Additional Guidelines for Conducting a Campaign in Secret

If you are currently employed, it will be difficult to participate in the TTP unless you use vacation time or take time off from your normal routine. However, if you can manage to practice TTP techniques to generate interviews, use the third-party approach. Start your conversation, as in a third-party sales letter, with "I have a friend who . . ." or "I know someone who. . . ." After interest has been established you can reveal yourself as the job candidate. If a PE requests information by mail, keep your identity secret until an interview is confirmed.

Regardless of what technique you use, you must be extremely careful of what you say about yourself until you are ready to drop your cover. Unusual experiences or assignments can be particularly revealing. You must either omit these items from communications with a PE—even though they would add to your presentation—or disguise them in such a way as to make them innocuous. For example, if you earned a Ph.D. in Paraguay, don't mention the school or country in describing your education. If you are the only one in your industry who has worked in China, either do not indicate where you obtained your experience or describe it as "experience in the Far East."

In general, you can trust PEs to keep your file confidential. But it takes only one exception—one PE getting back to your current employer—to endanger your security. For this reason, you should make it clear to every PE that you do not want anyone contacted until you have a firm offer. To make sure that your wishes are followed, do not release the names of former employers until you have an offer and are interested in going to work for the PE.

Use descriptions instead of names. For example, if you must fill out an employment form, describe your present company as "a major firm in the garment industry" or "a small independent petroleum company." Do the same with former employers. For your references, write descriptions of their present office or function: "manufacturing manager of a large company" or "past president of the American Bar Association." Finally, note on the application that you will provide names of companies and individuals after mutual interest has been established, and that you do not wish your present employer, references, or anyone else contacted until that time.

The Story of Engineer X

Engineer X was a bright, experienced engineer who once worked for me. He was doing well and as far as I knew was happy with his assignment. One day, out of the blue, I received a form letter from the personnel manager of a large company in the East. The letter stated that Engineer X was being considered for a job and asked me to fill out a detailed questionnaire on his salary, qualifications, and duties and my opinion of his performance.

When I questioned Engineer X, I was surprised to learn he had specifically requested that his present company not be contacted until he had accepted an offer. At the time I received the form letter, no offer had been made. Since I am an executive who believes that employees are not showing disloyalty by trying to better their job situation, no punitive action was taken. But it is an unpleasant fact that such unauthorized inquiries are made. The burden is on the executive job hunter to take the necessary precautions.

Adjusting the Length of Your Campaign

A campaign conducted in secret will take longer than one conducted in the open. Because you are fully occupied during normal working hours, you must spend evenings and weekends on your campaign. Your unemployed competitors have two major advantages. They can spend eight hours or more on their campaign every day, and they are highly motivated to get a job as soon as possible. Such a competitor can beat you out of a superior job if you are not careful.

But do not be dismayed if you are employed and must conduct your campaign in secret. If you are careful and take the precautions I discussed in this chapter, it is unlikely that your present employer will find out about your search. There is no sadder sight than an unhappy executive who plods along for years in a job he detests because he is afraid he will be fired if he looks for another job.

Don't let fear of losing your present position keep you from getting a superior job. Take the necessary precautions and work hard on your campaign. If you do, you will be able to find a superior job within a reasonable time without jeopardizing your present position.

11

The Advantages
of Being Unemployed

It's no fun being unemployed, and many employment counselors will advise you to hold on to your job at any cost. But the fact remains that unemployed job hunters enjoy distinct advantages over their employed competitors. These advantages include: time, freedom of action, lack of conflict of interest, and determination and a sense of urgency.

How to Take Advantage of Time

Time refers to the total period that you spend on your campaign, from initial planning to accepting a superior job offer. This book outlines a ten-week campaign. During this period, if you are unemployed, you can concentrate all your efforts on your campaign. You have at least eight hours a day that a significant number of your competitors do not have. This time will be of tremendous help to you. Without difficulty, you can devote a minimum of 45 hours per week to your campaign.

In contrast, if you are employed, you will have to divide your attention between your campaign and your job. It will be extremely difficult, both practically and psychologically, to work as hard as your unemployed competitors. In fact, it is unlikely that you will do so. In order to put in 45 hours a week on your campaign, you would have to work from six to eleven every night plus 20 hours every weekend.

Thus time is a tremendous ally if you are unemployed. You have it. Your unemployed competitor does not.

The Importance of Freedom of Action

If you are currently employed, your freedom of action is limited by the responsibilities of your job. You will have difficulty scheduling interviews and talking on the phone with PEs during working hours. Furthermore, a PE may ask you if your employer knows that you are seeking a new job. Such a question is difficult to answer. A "no" implies disloyalty, while a "yes" indicates that your employer intends to let you go soon anyway. Or the PE may ask if you are taking company time for the interview. To win with this question, if you aren't interviewing after hours, on weekends, or on a holiday, you had better be on vacation.

If you are unemployed, you are in no way committed to other responsibilities. You can interview any time you please, with complete freedom of action. You are free to allocate your time however you wish to support your job campaign. You are also spared the psychological strain of having to keep your actions secret from those around you.

The Importance of a Lack of Conflict of Interest

Your best chances in job hunting are with a direct competitor. That is, it will be easiest for you to find a job in a similar function, in the same industry, at the same or a slightly higher level, and in a similar-size company. But even though a competitor may be the best source for a superior job, the potential conflict of interest is obvious. If your present employer finds out that you have approached a competitor, your career may come to an abrupt halt if the potential job falls through. In discussing your background and performance with a PE, you must guard against disclosing competitive information. Your PE will also be extremely cautious. How much can he afford to tell an executive of a competing company? And if you get an offer, are you wanted for your ability or for your immediate knowledge of the PE's competition?

The same is true to some extent if you are unemployed, but the danger is reduced. Even if you've been out of work a week, your old company has had the opportunity to take internal action to guard against your going with the competition. You are no longer privy to inside knowledge and decisions at your company. The competition knows this. If you are unemployed, you are "fair game" to rival firms. Your actions in conducting your job campaign cannot in any way be construed as disloyal or as a conflict of interest.

The Importance of Determination and a Sense of Urgency

In job hunting determination and a sense of urgency are more important than you might think. This doesn't mean that you need a "killer instinct" or cutthroat aggressiveness to find a superior job. It does mean that you must maintain pressures on yourself and your PEs throughout your campaign. Many executives find it difficult to do this when they are comfortably employed on a salary. How often have you heard unhappy executives complain for years about their present job and talk about leaving without ever taking action? The term "wage slave" describes it pretty well.

When you are unemployed, you know that you must get a job and you are determined. You have a sense of urgency because you know that you have no alternative except to find a new position. These two qualities, coupled with a positive mental attitude, will assist you in finding a superior job in the shortest possible time.

The Critical Thing You Must Do If You Are Unemployed

One critical thing you must do if you are unemployed is to decide, with your former employer, on a mutually acceptable reason for your leaving. You must discuss this with your old employer, and the reason must be specific and acceptable to a PE. "It just wasn't working out" is neither specific nor acceptable. "It wasn't working out because there was more travel associated with the job than I expected" is good as long as you don't intend to look for a job that requires a lot of travel. A personality conflict with your immediate supervisor is all right, but a little dangerous. If you go this route, you should line up other supervisors who are ready to volunteer that you are easy to get along with.

Be truthful but creative. Make certain that you have your old employer's complete agreement on the reason you give. And remember, you needn't volunteer this information to a PE. But you should have it ready in case you are asked, and the reason should check out easily.

Throughout this book I have stressed allowing for your competition in finding a superior job, because in the real world of the job market that is how it is. If you are unemployed, the advantages of time, freedom of action, lack of conflict of interest, and determination and sense of urgency are yours. If you capitalize on them and use the techniques discussed in this book, you will be able to find your superior job in ten weeks.

12

How to Use
Friends Effectively
in Your Campaign

Friends and Acquaintances Can Help You in Your Campaign

Friends and close acquaintances can be of help in finding a superior job, but they should be used with caution. In fact, every contact made through a friend should be weighed well beforehand, for there are disadvantages as well as advantages to using this approach.

Let's look at the plus side first. Friends and acquaintances already know your capabilities and personality. They may be prepared to assist you in your search and may be ready to hire you themselves. With these obvious advantages, it is a great temptation to conduct a campaign based entirely on friendship. But although such campaigns are sometimes successful, it is unwise to concentrate solely on your friends to help you.

Why You Must Not Conduct a Campaign Based Solely on Friendship

Just as only a small percentage of companies need your particular services at any given time, so only a small percentage of friends will be able to assist you in finding a position. Even if you have more than 100 friends, very few will know of openings that meet your job specifications.

Frequently, friends may be reluctant to hire you or recommend you for their company. They would much prefer to hire a stranger, who could be readily fired, transferred, or promoted as business interests dictate. Personal friendships make business relationships more difficult. Many executives prefer not to have people they know work for them or with them.

It is true that friends can get you interviews with PEs, but many of these meetings will be "courtesy interviews." In a courtesy interview a PE agrees to see you, not because he particularly wants to, but as a favor to your friend. For example, a friend of yours who is president of a company has nothing for you but does not want to disappoint you. So he calls a friend of his who is president of a second company. This second president meets with you and sends you to another executive in his company. You could spend a lot of time—your most important resource—following your friend's lead when a job opening doesn't even exist.

If you are employed and use friends to help you find a superior job, the secrecy of your campaign will be limited. The more people who know you are job hunting, the greater the chance that your campaign will get back to your present employer. Also, the mere fact that you contact PEs through friends can devalue your worth. Why is this? Most of your friends will not be talented salespeople. You have little or no control over how they present you to a PE. You may be described as a truly talented professional who is willing to listen if approached just right. But you are far more likely to be described as a good executive "who is looking," "who needs a job," or "who is out of work."

In job hunting you should not overlook any technique or lead that could result in a superior job offer. So despite the drawbacks, I recommend that you use friends in your campaign. Just be sure you proceed carefully and do not rely on contacts made through friends as your primary means of generating interviews.

The Two-Groups-of-Names Method for Using Friends

The two-groups-of-names method will enable you to use friends effectively in your campaign. First, sit down and make a list of people you know well who could assist you by hiring you themselves, recommending that you be hired, or referring you to openings for which you are qualified. These should be people who think highly of you and who have the highest probability of assisting you. This is group number one.

Next, make a list of people you do not know well who still make be able to help you in your campaign. It may be an executive you met one night at a cocktail party and had an hour's discussion with. He works in your functional area at a higher level, but you really can't call him a close friend. Or it could be someone you have met several times through your work but do not know intimately. This is group number two.

Contact these executives at home after hours. Since you have only a couple of hours each evening to make your calls, you will probably be able to talk to no more than six people each day. Start with the first group, those who have a higher probability of helping you. Tell them your situation in detail, including why you want to leave or have left your old job. Do not indicate that you are in any way desperate, even if you think you are. Any negative feelings you convey will be passed on to PEs. As always, speak with confidence and adopt a positive mental attitude.

Tell your friend that even though you are interested in a new job, your services are in demand. Describe some of the accomplishments listed in your sales letter. Don't be hesitant about "tooting your own horn." You can't afford to be embarrassed to talk about your accomplishments when you are looking for a new job. In any case, you are simply stating facts to give your friend an idea of whether he or someone he knows can use you. You are not bragging about what you can do; you are objectively stating what you have already done.

Be enthusiastic and positive, but not arrogant. Your way lies down the middle—neither arrogant nor humble. Just let your friend know that you have done an outstanding job before and will undoubtedly do an outstanding job again for another company. Be certain to tell your friend if your job campaign is confidential.

Move on to your second group of names, those people you do not know well who may be able to help you. Be more cautious with this group. Give your full name and recall the circumstances of how you met. Explain that you are seeking a new position and have a unique background that the person may not be aware of. Mention why you thought of calling. From your motivation on, use the TTP techniques described in Chapter 7.

How to Identify Courtesy Interviews and What to Do About Them

I have already described courtesy interviews and why you should avoid them. The problem is, if you use friends in your campaign, you will be invited on some courtesy interviews. What should you do about them? Some executives interview so well that they can turn even a courtesy interview around and come up with a job offer. If you are such an individual, you should obviously pursue every lead you get, including courtesy interviews.

If you are the average executive job hunter, you should screen interviews coming in from friends. Some interviews will obviously be due to courtesy. Your contact will say something like, "Joe Doaks, an acquaintance of mine, who is manager of proposal preparation with United Steamrollers, doesn't have any openings now, but he would be happy to meet you when you have the time in case something should develop." Or your contact could say, "I really don't have anything right now, but why don't you drop by the office when you get in my area and we'll have lunch together and talk." Both these invitations are probably for courtesy interviews. Don't turn them down, and certainly don't let on that you think that only a courtesy interview is being offered. Just thank your contact and say that you will call for an appointment when you are able. Take time for these interviews only when you have nothing better to do in your campaign.

Other invitations for interviews coming from friends will not be as clear cut: "My friend Mary Anne is president of Advance Enterprises. I really don't know if she has anything for you, but she would definitely like you to call for an appointment." Or "Can you get downtown to my office tomorrow? I don't know if it means anything, but I told my boss about you and he wants to meet you." Both these invitations should be accepted, even though they could turn out to be for courtesy interviews. Sometimes a little probing with TTP techniques will help you classify the kind of interview you are being invited to.

Once you meet with your friend's contact, he may say something like, "Well, I really don't have anything right now, but I thought it worthwile that we get together in case something should come up." As soon as you have established beyond doubt that you are in a courtesy interview and that nothing is in the offing, ask your interviewer if he knows of an opening elsewhere or knows someone you can contact who might. Many interviews that you develop through this "pyramiding" technique will also be courtesy interviews, so you must continue to screen. However, others can lead to solid interviews and job offers, especially when you make good use of TTP techniques.

Pick Up the Challenge of Every Interview

Your ratio of job offers to interviews will probably be lower with friends than with other methods of getting interviews. This is normal, so don't be discouraged. You should continue to interview. If you work at every interview, you will find yourself getting better. Pick up the challenge and try to get the PE to make you an offer. View every interview as a training situation for improving your interviewing techniques. Even an interview that does not result in an offer will bring you closer to your goal.

If a friend suggests that you call someone for an interview, use your friend's name as an opener, but be certain to follow TTP techniques. Never say that you are calling because your friend suggested that the PE might have an opening. Do not say that you are looking for a job. Open with something like this: "Hello, Bob Douglas? This is Jim Jones. Dick Wood asked me to call." Then lead into your sales letter in the manner described in Chapter 7.

Why You Must Never Be a Job Applicant

There is a difference between a job applicant and a job candidate. An applicant applies for a job; a candidate is a contender for a job. You are ill advised to view yourself as an applicant for a job. Until you have had the interview, you can't possibly know enough about the job to tell if you are interested in applying for it. In fact, if you follow the instructions in this book, you will never be an applicant, because the job will be offered to you before you can apply for it.

You may think this is splitting hairs, but viewing yourself as a "candidate" rather than an "applicant" will make a difference in your job campaign. When you use friends to assist in job hunting and talk to strangers who have been recommended to you, a positive mental attitude is essential. You should not forget what you are or where you fit into the scheme of things.

How Al P. Found a Superior Job with Help from His Friends

Al P. of Los Angeles used friends in his job campaign to great advantage. Al was an aerospace engineer who found himself laid off during the recession of the early 1970s. A friend got Al an interview with the manager of his specialty in another aerospace company. As Al said later: "It was more or less a courtesy interview. He had the budget to hire someone, but there really wasn't an opening." Al followed the techniques for good interviewing and made such an impression that he got an immediate offer at roughly his old salary level. But Al went all the way. Never revealing his previous salary, Al succeeded in negotiating a salary 15 percent higher than the original offer.

There are many ways of generating interviews. Don't overlook any of them if they can be profitably integrated into your campaign plan. If you utilitze your friends' assistance in the ways described in this chapter, you can certainly find a superior job with their help.

13

The Concentration Strategy

The concentration strategy as described in this chapter is not for everyone. In fact, you should think very carefully before you decide to adopt it. It is much riskier than any other strategy recommended in this book. Furthermore, you should not consider attempting it unless you are already a skilled job finder with good general communication skills and the ability to interview very well at the outset. However, if the above description applies to you and you are willing to accept the risks, the concentration strategy can have a higher payoff in finding a superior job than any other method.

Now, you may expect that the concentration strategy is radically different, and it is; but the techniques that you use are not. In fact, the techniques in general are identical with those described previously. The radical difference in the concentration strategy, however, is that you concentrate all your resources, all your time, and all your efforts on obtaining one single superior job that you have decided you want.

How the Concentration Strategy Was Developed

The concentration strategy was developed through the efforts of a classmate of mine who picked up the initial edition of *The Executive's Guide to Finding a Superior Job* when he was out of work. This talented person, whom we will call Ed, had a most unusual background that began with his graduation from the United States Military Academy at West Point. During his ninth year of military service, his second tour of combat duty ended when he was severely wounded in Vietnam. He spent the next six months in the hospital and then was discharged from the Army. From the Army Ed bummed around Europe for a while, ending up in Greece as a sponge fisherman for a year, and then returned to the United States. He enrolled as an MBA student in a western university, and on completion was hired by a small company starting a chain of health food stores. Ed was successful in building this chain for a year or so, then left this operation for one of a series of entrepreneurial activities. At that time he met a young executive of about his own age (he was then in his late thirties or early forties) who was the chief financial officer of a major corporation listed by the New York Stock Exchange. This kindred spirit convinced Ed to come aboard as a director of new business development in what was to be his longest stint with a large company up to that time: one and a half years. This period of relative quiet in Ed's career ended when both he and his friend were fired because someone discovered that they were apparently trying to take over the company.

Ed then reentered the realm of entrepreneurship, and he and his friend co-authored and self-published a book on entrepreneurship.

The Challenge

At the time that Ed obtained *The Executive's Guide to Finding a Superior Job,* he was between activities and his money was beginning to run out. He called me immediately after reading my book, highly excited about the techniques described in it, and he stated that he had seen the one and only job that he wanted advertised in *The Wall Street Journal* that very day. He asked if he might come to my home to discuss it with me. I agreed.

Ed entered my den with a fragment of a torn piece of *The Wall Street Journal* grasped in his hand. On it was advertised the job Ed wanted: vice president of a division of a major motion picture studio. Needless to say, I was somewhat surprised.

Ed asked whether it was possible for him to obtain this job. Now, the opening was for a vice president of new business development, and Ed had been director of new business development with the only other large company he had been with. Also, new business development implies a certain background of entrepreneurship credentials, which Ed held in spades. However, the chances of his getting one single great job like this were very small. I explained to Ed that while it was possible, he faced considerable risk of failure and that perhaps if he wanted to be a company officer with this title in a major company, a mailing to a number of companies might be a better route than relying on only this one job opening. However, Ed was not to be deterred, and as his friend I decided to help him.

Clearly, Ed already had a positive mental attitude, and he also had defined his personal professional objective explicitly. What he did have to do, however, was to plan his job campaign, develop a superior resume, and decide on the exact strategy that should be used to approach this job opportunity.

Ed and I spent several hours together going over his background in some detail, establishing all his experiences, and documenting them as accomplishments (as was recommended to you in an earlier chapter). After some probing, we came up with some impressive achievements. For example, he had started up a new concept for a beverage and had already sold 100,000 cases before it was even manufactured. A marketing plan he had developed for the major corporation that he'd worked for had been implemented and had resulted in the company's stock increasing by 300 percent. And, of course, he was co-author of a book on entrepreneurship.

The Strategy

We decided on using a third-party campaign strategy rather than simply responding to the advertisement and the personnel manager listed. Acting as third party, I would find out to whom the position reported, speak with this person, and attempt to get an interview or at least learn all that was possible about the job, as described earlier in this book.

I called the major motion picture studio and asked for the name of the president of the appropriate division of the studio. I then asked for him, spoke to him myself, and said that I had a friend who had learned about the opening for this particular position as a vice president and wanted to know more. In this way I found out more about what the job required than was revealed in the advertisement. I also described, just as indicated in the chapter on getting an interview through the telephone, some of Ed's outstanding accomplishments. The president of the division, let's call him Jim, agreed that my classmate sounded like a good candidate. However, he also advised me that the hiring was being handled through his personnel manager. I then suggested that Ed send a letter describing his qualifications to Jim with a copy to the personnel manager, Joe.

After my conversation with Jim I called Joe, telling him that I had spoken with Jim and that Ed was sending a letter directly to Jim describing his qualifications and that he, Joe, would be receiving a copy. At that time Joe advised me that they had received 500 resumes (not letters) in response to their advertisement so far.

Ed developed his letter, which was written in the format recommended in this book for responding to advertisements, but mentioning my conversation with Jim.

Several weeks later Ed got a call from the personnel manager. He was invited to come in for a preliminary interview. At this point I advised Ed to implement the techniques on how to interview effectively, which he did. However, since he was going after only this one single job, he went to extraordinary lengths to find additional information. He used every single contact he had to get additional contacts, not only within the industry but also within the company, and to learn everything he possibly could about this particular job as well as what would be expected of the vice president for new business development. Ed went to the extent of making telephone calls around the country for information. By the date of the interview he was very well primed.

This preliminary screening interview was with Joe, the personnel manager. Ed learned that he was one of ten candidates who had been called in for this screening interview, out of more than 800 resumes that had been submitted to Joe for this position. Most had experience in the industry and almost all had been company officers, which Ed had not. Ed's was the only letter and one of the few of the 800 submissions that indicated neither industrial nor company officer experience. Even so, Ed thought that the interview had gone well.

Several weeks later Ed received an additional call. He was one of the five finalists and was invited in to meet various company officers, including his potential boss, Jim. Again, he went to extraordinary lengths to prepare, using the additional information he had obtained from Joe during his interview with him. Once more he felt that the interview session had gone well. It had been with four other company officers including his PE, Jim, and with the president of the major motion picture studio itself.

At this point I was removed from the picture, being called to active duty in the Air Force for approximately a month. On my return Ed called me again, saying that twice during my absence he had been called in for interviews with various executives and that to his knowledge he was still in the running. Furthermore, he had just been called by Joe to come in the following Tuesday. Although Joe hadn't said so, Ed expected that he was going to receive an offer, and he questioned me about what the salary might be.

On Tuesday I was teaching at night and so did not return until approximately 10:30. Ed called a few minutes later to announce that he had received the offer and had accepted it.

Why the Concentration Strategy Worked for Ed

Clearly, Ed's obtaining this job was a major personal accomplishment as well as confirmation of the effectiveness of the various techniques he had used. His experience demonstrates the advantages of concentrating everything on one single target. If you are successful in applying this unique strategy, the payoff can be incredibly high.

In analyzing the reasons for Ed's amazing success in obtaining this superior job, I think the following factors are important:

1. *Ed was extremely self-confident and had a positive mental attitude to begin with.* In his own mind there was no doubt whatsoever of his ability not only to do this job once he had obtained it but also to get the job and win out over his competitors, regardless of their qualifications.

2. *The techniques that Ed used were extremely effective.* They are the techniques that are discussed throughout this book.

3. *Ed didn't just do superficial planning.* He did detailed planning as to exactly what strategy he was going to use to get the job. This planning was not haphazardly done in any sense.

4. *Ed was willing to wait.* His efforts to obtain this one single job took, from start until the job offer, twelve weeks. During this time in which he was unemployed, he did little else except interview, make contacts, and get information pertaining to this one single job.

5. *Ed was willing to accept the consequences should the job fall through.* Along these lines I should mention that Ed had the advantage of not having a family dependent on his income.

Is This Strategy Right for You?

From Ed's case, it is clear that the concentration strategy can work. But before you decide to adopt it, you should not forget the disadvantages. The biggest disadvantage is the extreme risk. Any one of a hundred different factors can knock you out of contention for one single job. When you increase your chances by going after many of the same types of jobs that also meet your objectives, you create a situation where eventually you must succeed. However, for any single job, the odds of success are nowhere near as great.

Another disadvantage of going after only one job is that you have no time for a learning experience. You must be on target the first time, not only with your letter but also in any conversations on the telephone and with your interviewing as well. If you are not already skilled in these areas, you have no time to learn.

The ideal situation, as explained elsewhere in this book, is to be negotiating with several different companies simultaneously. In this way you, rather than they, maintain control; and you are in an optimum negotiating position both psychologically and in reality. However, when you are going after one job, this is not true. You have no other job offer to help you out psychologically with the peaks and the valleys of your campaign, nor do you have any hard evidence of other offers which you can use to bring pressure on your target company and your prospective employer to get an offer.

To summarize, the concentration strategy can work. It works because you are able to concentrate all your resources on one single target, something that your competitors will probably not do, even if you have 800 or even 1,000 of them. Therefore, without question, you will be an outstanding candidate for this job. On the other hand, because of the increased risks, the personal idiosyncrasies, and other strange happenings in any job-finding situation, there is considerable risk of your not succeeding.

14

Strategies for a Tough Job Market

There is an old saying that when the going gets tough, the tough get going. It is certainly true that in a tough job market it is time to pull out all stops and really get yourself in gear if you are going to get the superior job that you are capable of getting. Strangely, what is called for here is nothing all that extraordinary, but rather the nerve and energy to do what is required. In fact, most available tactics that could be used in a tough job market are not illegal but aren't used simply because most people don't have the chutzpah to use them. Winners do, and they march off with the superior jobs. However, some of these tactics are so outrageous that you yourself have to define where your ethics stand, and no one can do this for you since ethics themselves are a relative concept. Let me tell you what I am talking about here so that you may make a decision yourself as to what you ethically can and cannot do.

Get Information Any Way You Can

At one point in my own career as an executive for a company, it was decided to do some research into a product that we suspected was a growing market. Not having our own market researchers available in the company, we interviewed perhaps one of the most prestigious marketing research firms in the Los Angeles area. The information required in order to decide whether to get into this market included precise information as to sales, methods of distribution, and other questions that were clearly proprietary to the company that manufactured these items. During the initial interview with the market research firm, I expressed some concern about whether the researchers would be able to get the necessary information about the competition. The researcher working on the problem looked at me blandly and assured me they would have no difficulty in getting this information. I couldn't imagine how, because the majority of companies in this business were privately owned, and this meant that many normal secondary sources of research were closed. Yet, 30 days later, the researcher showed up with this information in precise detail. With some amazement and a great deal of innocence I asked how he could have possibly obtained it. He told me it had been simple. He had merely called up the president of each company concerned and identified himself as a student working on a project for a college business class. Ninety percent of the companies had given out all the information necessary, even though it was proprietary.

This sort of thing speaks volumes about the security that any company should maintain regarding anything worthwhile protecting. It also raises the question of ethics and points out that good ethics are relative. I later discovered that almost every marketing research firm may use similar tactics to obtain information if required as a part of a study. Let's look at a different example closer to home; an example of a technique that might actually be used by a job hunter under certain circumstances. I have seen this technique used by professional headhunters.

A new executive recruiter had been calling the presidents and vice presidents of various firms, asking them directly whether they would like to become clients of his headhunting firm. One vice president of engineering of a petroleum company had no business to give to this neophyte and was particularly rude and abusive about it. He stated not only that his firm did not use headhunters under any circumstances to obtain anyone, but that he refused to talk to headhunters, would allow none of his staff to talk to headhunters, and had threatened to fire any secretary or anyone speaking to headhunters. He then hung up.

The director of the division of the headhunting firm observed what had happened and told the new recruiter that this was the kind of firm to recruit from, in other words, to raid. He asked the new headhunter for the name and the telephone number of the executive he had just talked to. Less than five minutes after the conversation in which this vice president of engineering had insisted that he allowed no one to talk to headhunters, this director had the same person on the telephone and was talking with him, but not as a headhunter. He gave the cover story that he was a university student who had been asked to write a report about petroleum engineering and had been given the name of a petroleum engineer with whom to talk. "However," pleaded the director innocently, "I have forgotten the engineer's name and I am afraid to contact my professor to tell him this." The vice president of engineering then spent the next half hour identifying every single engineer in his company by name and by duty to this "student." At the end of this period the director even had the nerve to ask, "Are you sure that's every single engineer listed in your company?" And the vice president of engineering answered, "Well, everyone except me," and then gave his own name as well. The director then thanked the vice president of engineering, hung up, and presented the amazed neophyte with the names and titles of over 100 different engineers, all of whom were potential recruits for the headhunter's client firms.

I have seen other headhunters claim that they were trying to reach someone in the company whose fender they had dented, or say that they had promised to send a calendar to someone but could not remember the name. Through these tactics, headhunters find initial contacts who may unwittingly help them identify candidates potentially qualified for various jobs all the way from the first-line professionals up to very senior positions in management.

Such techniques can be used by anyone and are extremely valuable for obtaining intelligence about a company, which is useful in capturing a superior job. For example, if you could obtain the names of professionals that are working in a company, even if you didn't know them, you could call them and address them by name. You would then be able to ask questions about a position that is open (or one that may be open), about problems with the company, about ongoing problems for which company management is seeking solutions, and various other questions before you have the interview. Again, I don't comment on the ethics here. This is up to you as an individual to decide, but I do point out that these tactics are used frequently by recruiters. They can be adopted by you for integration into your own campaign in a tough job market. They are effective and will help you get a superior job.

Seek Two Kinds of Jobs Simultaneously

There is nothing written that will prevent you from applying for two entirely different jobs in different industries simultaneously. Everything depends here on your packaging, and the key to remember is that you must be a specialist. You cannot, for example, send out the same sales letter for two totally different jobs. Your packaging of your past experiences and background must be changed to emphasize one job or the other. But if you do this effectively, you can have a much wider range of jobs available when it is time to make your final decision about which job you want. You will also have more interviews, receive more job offers, and get a superior job much more quickly and probably under better terms than you otherwise might.

There are two ways of doing this. One is to write different letters for entirely different industries. For example, one executive job seeker conducted a successful campaign in which he sought a job as a director of engineering and simultaneously did a mailing seeking a position as a management consultant. Ultimately he chose a high-paying job as a management consultant. But the important thing to remember here is that he got much more exposure and interview experience, and when he finally made the decision to become a consultant he knew that this was the right route to go even though he did not immediately eliminate a potential job as a director of engineering.

Some of my own experiences illustrate just how far you can go here. At one point I decided to move into marketing management for a major aerospace company. I was perfectly willing to hold either of two jobs: vice president of marketing, or, failing this, marketing manager reporting directly to a vice president. Because the aerospace industry was in a recession at the time, I felt it wiser to not limit myself to the vice president's job. Accordingly, I wrote two slightly different letters, both emphasizing my marketing expertise, but one emphasizing my top-level management experience and the other not being quite so precise about what level of experience I had.

Now, what do you do in this case about disguising the name on the letter? After all, here I was applying for a vice president's job, which implied that I must write to the president; and at the same time I must write to the vice president of the same company in order to get the marketing manager's job. The two letters were alike, except for the stated job objective and the slant of the description of accomplishments. I used my full name and address with nothing changed. Eventually I got the job I sought, but on the way a funny thing happened. I'm including this story here as an encouraging case of a job candidate beating bureaucracy—and as an amusing example of the strange things that can happen in a campaign for a superior job.

I received a telephone call from the vice president of marketing of a major aerospace corporation saying that he had received my letter and requesting that I come in for an interview. I told my wife I was interviewing with this company and left for an interview at approximately ten o'clock in the morning. The interview went quite well, and I was taken out for lunch by the vice president of marketing and the executive vice president of the same company. Now, normally I am not much of a cocktail drinker at lunch, because drinking of any sort makes me very sleepy and I am unable to work well in the afternoon. (Incidentally, I would advise you not to partake of alcohol during interviews.) But at the end of lunch, my two hosts each ordered a double martini, and in order not to be different I had a double martini as well. We had no sooner finished our martinis when someone at another table said, "Another round for those three gentlemen over there," and we were soon looking at another double martini. By the time we left lunch, these two fellows thought I was the greatest candidate in the world, and I thought I'd rather work with them than with anyone else I'd ever met. I worried about my ability to drive home, but as I left the interview the vice president of marketing grasped my hand and said, "You're our kind of guy. We like you and you'll have an offer in the mail— and it will be one that you won't want to turn down."

I got into my car, managed to drive home, and was greeted by my wife—who looked at me with a rather suspicious eye. "I thought you went to an interview," she said, and she presented me with a letter from the company where I had just interviewed. The letter read something like this:

Dear Mr. Cohen:
    Mr. Jones, our president, has asked me to respond to your fine resume [which I didn't send] and to check our openings against your fine background. Unfortunately, there are no openings for someone of your outstanding qualifications at the present time. However, we are putting your resume [which I didn't send] in our permanent file [which I believe is round, is made of metal, and sits on the floor] and we will contact you the minute that an opening occurs. Thank you again for thinking of us.

                                                    Sincerely yours,

                                                    Personnel Manager

Upon reading this I started laughing because, as I informed my wife, the president of this company had been and was still in Europe for the past three weeks enjoying a hard-earned vacation. What had happened was that my letter addressed to the president had been screened out by the secretary and sent to personnel, and I had received the personnel manager's standard form-letter answer. By the way, I did get an offer from this company. If I hadn't received a better one from another firm where I had sent letters both to the president and to the vice president of marketing, I would have taken it.

This incident illustrates many different things. But it certainly emphasizes just how far you can go in your job campaign. You may wonder whether, in any firm, the vice president of marketing and the president ever talked about these two different letters which I had sent to the same company. The answer is yes. As a matter of fact, at the company that finally hired me, the president and the vice president of marketing had compared notes. What did they think? They thought it was rather clever. Maybe that's one reason I got the offer.

Create Your Own Job Out of Nothing

In many cases you may have a specific background and unique experiences and qualifications that enable you to see a need before it is recognized by a company. If you do identify such an unfulfilled need in a company, write a letter to the president about setting up and running a department to perform this function. Let me give you an example of this.

A friend of mine is a data analyst consultant within a large company, where she teaches executives how to make use of computers in their work. Even though the capabilities of computers and data processing in today's market are extensive, only a small percentage of executives are using these capabilities to anything approaching their full potential. Therefore, her job is to teach executives how to do this.

Although her company has recognized this need, many others have not. Even though computers are used as a daily part of their business and a special department exists to do their computing per se, there is no one that teaches executives about the new technology or consults with them on how their operation might be improved by the use of computers and data processing. Therefore, if this specialist wanted work in other companies, the opportunity exists for her to create her own job out of nothing and to become a department head simply by selling not only her accomplishments but also the unique advantages of the function.

This technique is especially useful when a function that has been recognized by very large companies can be adapted to smaller companies. This may be true in a case such as the data analyst consultant I already mentioned, but also in many other areas that small or medium-size companies may not yet have developed to full advantage. Two examples come to mind. A large company, in dealing with the government or other industrial firms, maintains large departments that do nothing but coordinate and write proposals for work. The same concept can be adapted for smaller companies; perhaps not an entire department, but one person could specialize in writing proposals. Since there are many advantages of doing this, this concept can be sold to medium-size or small companies. In the same way, very large companies frequently have employees whose function is to market the licensing of inventions that the company developed but for which it has no use. This occurs because many large companies, which may spend millions of dollars for research and development, develop products that have nothing to do with their main product line. Now, small companies may also spend money for research and development to develop new products, but on a much smaller scale, so that every dollar saved is important. This creates an opportunity for an employee whose responsibility is the reverse of those who market licenses in a larger company: to seek out inventions available from larger companies and to license them for manufacture. This could save a small company thousands of dollars in research and development.

Answer Every Ad with Two Letters

Most advertisements that are placed seeking executives to fill jobs advise the potential respondent to send a resume to a personnel manager. As pointed out in an earlier chapter, I don't recommend sending a resume or going along with other requirements of the advertisement, although I do recommend targeting the advertisement and concentrating your resources to respond to the specific requirements of the job. Another technique that you may use to double your chances involves writing two letters in response to every advertisement that appears attractive. One letter should be targeted in accordance with instructions given in Chapter 6. However, in a second letter, write to the person responsible for the hiring: the one you would actually report to. This means that you must first find out who that person is.

As mentioned previously, this is accomplished fairly simply by imagining to whom the job would report, by title, and asking a receptionist for the name. If you are seeking a job as a director of engineering or an engineering manager, chances are that this position reports to the vice president of engineering. Therefore, simply call the company in question and ask the receptionist who the vice president of engineering is. If the job is for a marketing manager, then clearly it must report to a vice president of marketing. Or, if the job is a top management job carrying a vice president's title, then it clearly must report to the president of the company. Once you get the name, proceed with the next step.

Now send one letter to the personnel address as indicated in the advertisement, and address the other to the executive who is your PE. In this letter you will say that you have learned about the company's need for a _____, and you will then, using the advertisement as assistance, write a sales letter emphasizing your accomplishments just as you were taught in Chapter 5.

This technique clearly increases your chances. At the very worst, the personnel manager will have two letters, one written directly to him as required by the advertisement and the other sent down from the person who may be interested in hiring you—sometimes with the notation, "I'd like to see this one," or something to that effect. Such a notation won't hurt a bit. But even without the notation, you have less chance of getting screened out.

Use Your Contacts in a Letter-and-Telephone Campaign

In Chapter 12 I showed you some techniques for using your friends effectively. As discussed, you can use contacts that you may have because you went to the same university, were in the same professional, fraternal, or athletic organization, or met in some other way. Get these people to give you the names of their contacts, whom you will approach yourself. Write to these PEs instead of having your friend or associate do it for you. This will strengthen the perception of you by the executive concerned and will also lessen the number of courtesy interviews that you may get, since the PE, if he does respond to your letter, will be inviting you in for a real interview rather than agreeing to interview you out of politeness to your friend. Your letter to such a PE should read something like this:

Dear _____:

I was speaking the other day with Joe Doaks, vice president of the ABC Company. He suggested that you might be able to help me with some problems that I am now having.

I recently resigned my position as _____ and am putting my career plans together. [Or, "Although I am fully employed, frankly I have decided to make some new career plans."]

Here are some of the things that I have done in the past.

[At this point you should use the bullet system and illustrate five or six different accomplishments related to the superior job that you have decided on.]

Although I certainly would be interested in talking with you about the possibility of joining your firm, I recognize that there may not be a suitable position open at the present time. However, I would still be very much interested and would appreciate the opportunity to talk with you. Therefore, I will call your office to request an appointment for a short interview.

Sincerely,

_____

Make certain that you call within two days. This letter will, of course, assist you in getting through the PE's secretary because you can tell the secretary that your call is expected. What should you do if the secretary says that your letter was received and was sent to personnel? Simply tell her that this must have been a mistake since you are not applying for a position. And again ask to be connected with the executive concerned. Once you get the executive, repeat that although you would appreciate being considered for a position, the primary reason for your desire to get together for a few minutes is to get advice regarding your career plans and not to seek a specific position in the company. This combination of using a contact plus a letter-and-telephone campaign is very effective for getting high-level interviews, especially in a tough job market.

The strategies and concepts illustrated in this chapter should be reviewed as indicative of what you can do to better your job-hunting odds when times are tough. There are only three things that should restrain you. One is the law. Do not do anything that is illegal. The second is your personal code of ethics. You have to decide what is ethical and what is not, and no one can do this for you. And third, you should never do anything that might be viewed as bizarre.

All the techniques described here involve actions that are concealed from your PE or actions that—even if your PE found out about them— would probably be viewed either as clever or as evidence of your aggressiveness in a positive way. However, bizarre or strange acts will not be viewed this way. For example, the number-one method of getting a job is, unquestionably, to use the direct mail campaign as illustrated and recommended in Chapter 5. One kind of direct mail campaign that works well in selling products is the lumpy package, because people almost always open letters that are lumpy simply to find out what is inside. However, your using such a technique in a mailing to PEs would be a bizarre strategy and would not be a good idea. Yes, your lumpy letter would probably be opened and you might even get a response; however, because the tactic is bizarre and not par for normal business practice, you would probably not get an interview—unless you were in the direct response industry, where this would be considered not at odds with the norm.

15

How to Interview Effectively

The interview is the payoff of all the actions taken thus far in your campaign. At the executive level virtually no one receives a job offer or gets hired without an interview. In this chapter I will show you how to interview successfully, how to control the interview so that it goes your way, and how to come out with a high percentage of job offers.

Two Principles of Interviewing That You Must Obey

There are two principles of interviewing that you must obey throughout your campaign. I say *must* obey because if you do not you will lose job offers and prolong your campaign. The first principle is never to turn down an interview (except for screening out obvious courtesy interviews, as described previously). At the interview you may learn additional facts that make the job more attractive to you. Further, your interviewing techniques and overall performance will improve with each interview. The more time you spend interviewing, the better you will be.

The second principle is to try to get the PE to extend you a job offer, even if you do not want the job. Why? First, you can always turn an offer down after it has been made. But if you don't make an honest effort to get an offer during an interview, you usually cannot get the PE to extend the offer later. Second, if you make a practice of not trying for a job during the interview, you will be developing the wrong attitude. You will not command all the interviewing skills you need. Practice getting the PE to offer you the job. Then when you find the superior job you really want, you will have the skills you need to get the offer.

How Richard C. Got a Superior Job He Could Have Lost

Richard C. was an out-of-work accountant. About three weeks into his job campaign he had an outstanding interview for a job as senior accountant. In the meantime Richard was invited in for an interview with another company. It too was for a good job. Richard was so certain of being offered the first job that he considered telling company number two that he really wasn't interested.

Fortunately, Richard remembered both principles of interviewing. He went into the second interview pretending that the first interview had never taken place, and he went after the second job offer in earnest. It was a good thing that Richard did. Not only did he discover some facts that made the second offer better than the first, but the first job offer failed to materialize. Richard had an immediate backup offer that he accepted. Today, five years later, he is a vice president with company number two.

What Information You Should Get Before the Interview

The interview should begin long before it takes place face to face. In fact, it begins with your first contact with the PE. As pointed out in earlier chapters, in your initial telephone conversation you should try to learn as much as you can about the job, the PE, and the individuals you will be working with. If the invitation for the interview comes to you by mail, you must take the initiative and make the telephone contact to get additional information.

Before the face-to-face interview, you should ask the PE for a full description of the position (including why it is available) and a description of the qualities the PE is looking for. You should also find out what happened to the individual who previously held the job, whom the position reports to, and who you will interview with besides the hiring executive.

To get additional information before the interview, talk to anyone in the hiring company who might help. Ask questions casually, as you engage the other party in conversation. Get as much information as you can, but don't push. If the individual refuses to answer a question, give way. Then proceed with some other questions. Always be pleasant and courteous. Do not under any circumstances get into an argument with a representative of the PE, even if you are provoked.

Do not be offended if the hiring executive does not make the initial contact. The hiring executive may be very busy and may ask someone else to call you to schedule an interview or to see if you are worth talking to. Use this opportunity to get all the preinterview intelligence you can. Frequently you will get valuable information that will assist you during the interview in presenting yourself as that unique candidate who fits all the PE's needs. However, keep in mind that your objective in the initial phone conversation is not to reveal information about yourself, it is to obtain additional information about the job and the PE.

What to Do After Setting Up the Interview

After setting up the interview and getting as much information as you can, you should do some research on the company and the executives you will be meeting. One good source is Standard & Poor's *Register of Corporations, Directors, and Executives.* You can also get information on your PE from your bank or brokerage house, the PE's annual report, *Fortune's* 500 listing, Moody's manual, Dun & Bradstreet's directories, a company's 10K report from the Securities and Exchange Commission, and special editions of trade magazines such as *Plastics* for the plastics industry, *Iron Age* for metals, and *Oil and Gas* for petroleum. You should go through recent editions of trade magazines, *The Wall Street Journal,* and the business sections of major newspapers for changes and developments in a firm.

For the executives you are going to meet, you should find out about education and schools, industrial and other experience, and hobbies. For the company, you should get information on products, annual sales, recent achievements, recent problems, acquisitions, and divestitures.

Why You Must Prepare a List of Questions Beforehand

The success of the interview will depend to a large degree on what you do beforehand. One essential task is to prepare a list of questions that you will ask during the interview. These questions should be designed to reveal your background and achievements in areas where you know the company is interested.

For example, in your research you may discover that a significant portion of the PE's business involves selling microwave coaxial cable components to the Navy and that the PE has had a great deal of trouble with quality control. If you have a quality control background, write down a question pertaining to this problem that will reveal your expertise in this area. For example: "I understand you have had some reliability problems with your microwave coaxial cable components. Was this an engineering problem or some problem with quality control?" If your background is in marketing, you can ask this leading question: "I understand that you sell microwave coaxial cable components to the Navy. Has marketing been any help in straightening out the quality control problems that you've had?"

Get the PE to talk about his problems. Once you are on the subject, continue to ask intelligent questions. These questions will indicate three things to the PE without your having to say them: (1) you know something important about the PE's company and appreciate his problems; (2) you have experience in areas that the PE is interested in; and (3) you are an expert in these areas.

You should also make a list of questions about the PE's recent successes. If sales have risen markedly over the previous year, ask how the increase was achieved. If the company has made a new acquisition, ask about the general philosophy behind it and whether the company plans to expand. Ask similar questions about declines in sales and divestitures. Formulate a list of questions pertaining to your specialty that you can use in all your interviews. These questions will help to establish your credibility as an expert in your field.

You should use your notes on the PE's executives to help establish rapport, build empathy, relate your background to the interviewing executive, and avoid pitfalls. Look for common interests. Maybe you went to the same school as the hiring executive, were in the same branch of military service, worked for the same company, or worked in the same industry.

If you have something in common, bring it up during the interview: "I hear that you worked for the XYZ Company. I was with them back in 1965." If you are going to be interviewed by the president and discover that you and he have a similar functional background, use this information. Mention it directly if you can, or try to couch your questions and answers in the terms of that specialty. Obviously you should avoid statements that are critical of that specialty.

If you are going to an interview with a company about whose product you know very little, you must spend enough time to acquire at least some specialized knowledge about that product. That is precisely how Allen S. got his superior job. Allen had spent the largest part of his career selling radio communications equipment. His interview was with a company developing, manufacturing, and marketing computer peripheral equipment. Allen managed a very successful interview, which ultimately led to a job offer, because in addition to his other qualifications Allen appeared very knowledgeable about the computer peripheral industry. He had spent several hours at his local library boning up on the subject before his interview. Even though Allen said that he had no experience selling computer equipment when he was asked, his questions were to the point and phrased in correct terminology. There was no question in the PE's mind that what Allen didn't know he could learn very rapidly. You must do the same thing Allen did if you are going to an interview with a company that makes a product with which you have had little experience.

What You Should Get from Your Preinterview Research

After you finish your preinterview research, you should have a well-thought-out list of questions that reveal your general knowledge of the company and its product and your knowledge of your specialty and how it applies to the PE's business. In addition, you should have a list of questions to ask toward the end of your interview if you are fairly certain you have made a sale. These questions are for your protection. Your prospective employer invites you in for an interview to determine if you can do the job. You must determine whether the position meets your job objectives. To do this, you should ask the PE for a detailed description of the position and its specific responsibilities. You should also find out what advanced training is available or required and what growth potential the position has.

You must not at this point ask questions about salary, fringe benefits, health insurance plans, or retirement plans. Defer such questions until you know you will be made a firm offer.

Do not rely on memory or scraps of paper in the interview. Write each question down in a small looseleaf notebook so you can combine earlier information on a PE with notes you take during the interview. If you use a notebook that fits inside your pocket, you will not need to carry a briefcase.

How to Handle Stress Interviews

You will find that most interviewers are other executives, "good guys" who will do everything they can to treat you professionally and put you at ease. However, every so often you will meet an interviewer who believes that putting a job candidate under stress is the most effective way to evaluate him. This type of interview can be sheer torture, but if you are ready for it, you will have an opportunity to look much better than your competition.

Stress can be generated by the interviewing environment, by the way qustions are asked, and by the questions themselves. You will not be able to control most factors in the environment. For example, a PE may have several interviewers talk with you simultaneously. The best way to handle this is to speak slowly, listen carefully, and answer only one question at a time. If an interviewer asks a question too rapidly or directly on the heels of someone else's question, ask him to repeat it. Above all, use the techniques described in this chapter to gain control of the interview.

A few interviewers will try such gross tactics as seating you so that the sun shines directly in your eyes. If this happens, ask politely if you can change your seat to avoid the sun. Never be afraid to tell the interviewer that you are uncomfortable and to explain why. If the heat has been turned up and your interviewer has removed his jacket, ask if the heat can be turned down or if you can remove your jacket as well. Be pleasant and tactful, but don't become intimidated.

You cannot do much about the way an interviewer asks questions except to ask him to repeat a question if you did not understand it. Never allow yourself to get angry during an interview, regardless of the provocation.

You can do something about questions that cause stress. Prepare yourself for likely stress questions by working out good, solid answers beforehand. Here are some typical stress questions that you should be prepared to answer *before* you go into an interview. Think up some of your own as well.

Where do you want to be five years from now? Where do you think you'll be?
Are you technical or management oriented? Why?
Why should we be interested in hiring you?
What's wrong with your present job?
Does your present employer know you are out looking for a job?
Why have you been laid off so many times?
Why have you made so many job changes?
Why are you interested in our company?
Are you ambitious?
Will you be out to take my job?
What are your three greatest strengths?
What are your three greatest weaknesses?
What do you think of our operation?

Why do you want to work here?
Do you feel you have top management potential? Why?
Are you a good manager?
Are you a good leader?
What have you disliked most about past jobs?
What do you think you would like best about this job?
If you were just graduating from school and starting your career, what
    would you do differently from what you have done?
Are you willing to relocate?
How important to you is salary versus other aspects of the job?
What five things have you done in your life (or career) that you are
    most proud of?
What does the term *success* mean to you?
What types of jobs are you looking for?
If you had your choice of any job at all at this moment, what would that
    job be and why?
Why aren't you making more money?
Where did you stand in your class in college? Why didn't you stand
    higher?
Why haven't you accomplished more?
How have you managed to accomplish so much?

Think about answers to these questions. Then practice your interview with
a friend, and ask your friend what you are doing right and what needs
polish. Role playing as practice for an interview can be extremely helpful. If
you have a videotape machine or at least a tape recorder to help you, so
much the better. Work at it until you can deliver your answers smoothly
and confidently. Before going into any interview, you should be so well
prepared that no unusual situation, strange environment, or stress question can shake you or cause you to be ill at ease.

Mental Rehearsal Will Help You Win at the Interview

Psychologist Charles A. Garfield interviewed 1,200 top performers in
all fields. One characteristic that clearly set apart top-performing chief
executive officers was their ability to mentally rehearse coming actions or
events. As reported by *The Wall Street Journal* on January 13, 1982:

- Mr. Garfield says he was most surprised by the trait of mental rehearsal,
  now a popular concept in sports. Top chief executives imagined every facet
  and feeling of what would have to happen to make a presentation a

success, practicing a kind of purposeful daydreaming. A less effective executive, he says, would prepare his facts and agendas but not his psyche.

When I read this article, I realized that I had been practicing mental rehearsal for some years without realizing it. You may have also. The major use I've made of this technique is for speeches. No matter how many times you climb a platform, looking out at your audience can be a bit unnerving. Practicing mental rehearsal lets me get rid of my nervousness during the rehearsal. Also, the rehearsal is much faster and can be done at any time or in any place, and thus in some ways it is more valuable than a real rehearsal. Since last January, I have recommended mental rehearsal for job interviews, and the feedback I am getting is quite good. I would definitely recommend that you try it.

Additional Hints for Meeting with Your PE

It goes without saying that you should not be late for an interview. On the other hand, it is unwise to be too early. If you are, you may give your PE the impression that you are too eager for the position. You want the PE to know that you are enthusiastic and interested in the job. You do not want the PE to feel that you are desperate. I recommend that you arrive no more than five minutes early.

Psychologists have discovered that the most critical period of the interview is the first *few* minutes. It is during this time that the PE decides whether to offer you a job. The remainder of the interview merely reinforces the original decision.

If first impressions really count that much (and they do), then personal appearance is extremely important. Follow these guidelines: Always be well groomed. Dress fashionably but conservatively. Men should wear a suit and tie. Women should also wear a suit, or a conservative skirt and blouse. Do not wear frayed shirts, old shoes, or any other worn clothing. Do not wear bowties, mod watches, or sunglasses. Men's chances of being offered a position will be reduced if they have exceptionally long hair, a beard, or a crewcut—unless their PE has the same.

Act relaxed, friendly, and enthusiastic. Call the interviewer by name. If you have established a first-name relationship, as suggested in the TTP, call your PE by his first name. If you have not, introduce yourself thus: "Mr. Smith, I'm Jim Jones. It's good to meet you." State both your first and last name. If the PE gives his first name, you may use it during the interview.

Generally it is advantageous to get on a first-name basis with your PE as soon as possible. However, some executive job hunters find this unnatural and uncomfortable. If you feel better about being more formal with the PE, do so. And whether you use first names or not, always treat the PE with respect, but not fear or awe.

In general, it is better not to smoke during the interview. If the interviewer doesn't smoke, he could take offense. If he just quit or is trying to quit, your smoking will not make for a very relaxed meeting. Finally, even if the PE smokes, he could interpret your smoking as a sign of nervousness.

As in any presentation (and an interview is a type of presentation), one key to success is your enthusiasm. You must be enthusiastic. If you are not enthusiastic about yourself, you cannot expect a PE to be very enthusiastic about you.

How to Gain Control of the Interview

A basic principle of good interviewing is to get the PE to do most of the talking. Your job is to impress the PE with your brilliance by the quality of your questions, not by a soliloquy of your abilities. To do this, you must capture the initiative subtly, without threatening your PE.

The first moments of the interview will probably be devoted to small talk. You may be asked about how easily you found the PE's office, the weather, your neighborhood, and so forth. If you wish, you can participate in these preliminaries. Comment on something you have in common with the interviewer (maybe you heard that the PE has the same hobby as you), an object in the PE's office, or whatever. This phase of the interview can be very important. You and the PE are sizing each other up. The PE is beginning to form a decision about you, just as you are forming your own attitudes toward the PE.

You must listen carefully for the moment when the preliminaries are over and the serious part of the interview begins. Often, the PE will say something like, "Well, we'd better get on with it," or "Tell me about yourself." You should say something like, "Certainly, but before we start, may I ask you a question?" Stop and wait for the PE to assent. Then ask, "Can you tell me the main qualifications for the job for which I am interviewing?"

As soon as the PE begins to answer, take out your notebook and begin to write. As soon as the PE is finished, go on to the next question and the next. Your objective in using this technique is to impress the PE with your qualifications by the quality of your questions. Also, you want to learn all you can about the job so that when you are asked to describe your experience and accomplishments—either during the interview or in a post-interview resume—you can tailor them to the requirements of the job.

If for any reason you have not been able to learn beforehand what job the PE has in mind, you should listen especially carefully. At some point the PE will say, "The reason I asked you in is. . . ." If the PE fails to give a reason for inviting you to the interview, try to get him to reveal it by saying, "Since you invited me in for this interview, I gather you have need for a _____." Or you could ask, "Is your need for a _____ due to expansion?" You must get the PE to discuss the reason for the interview so that you can better understand his problem. Remember, this is your last chance to get information that will enable you to present your background, accomplishments, and other qualifications as the obvious (but unstated) solution to the PE's problem.

Always avoid giving responses that could disqualify you for the job. Keep the initiative by asking questions and allowing the PE to do most of the talking. But be flexible. Occasionally you will find a PE who is determined to ask the questions himself. Let him. But take advantage of every opportunity to demonstrate your knowledge of the company and the interviewing executive or to state experiences that are obviously suited to the PE's needs. If you temporarily lose the initiative because the PE raises a question, answer the question, then recapture the initiative by asking a question of your own. If the PE says, "Tell me about yourself," ask which experience he is most interested in. This will help you in your answer. Here are some other questions you might want to ask:

Why are you going outside the company to fill this position?
Whom would I be replacing? Why is that person leaving?
If I am offered this position and accept it, exactly what will be expected of me?
What is the number-one priority for the executive who fills this job?

If the interviewer is doing most of the talking, you have control and the interview is going well. This does not mean that you sit like a bump on a log responding to questions in monosyllables. It does mean you do less talking because the PE is busy answering your astute and well-thought-out questions.

How to Avoid Salary Questions Before You Have Made a Sale

You should not discuss salary until you know that the PE is definitely interested in hiring you. The decision to extend an offer is made fairly early in the interview; compensation is not determined until much later. A figure that may be considered too high or even out of the question early in the interview may be perfectly acceptable after you have made a sale. Forcing the salary decision too soon may cause the PE to reject you at the start. During the rest of the interview the PE may simply go through the motions, barely listening to what you are saying. Giving a salary figure that is too low can also work against you, since the hiring executive may not consider you "heavy" enough for the job. Once a negative reaction has set in, it is very difficult to overcome.

The only solution is to postpone any discussion of salary until you have made your case and the PE wants to hire you. To do this, you must be prepared to fend off salary questions. If the PE asks what you are currently making or what compensation you are seeking, put him off with one of the following:

- "Like you, I do not have a definite salary figure in mind. However, after we discuss some of the requirements of the job, I'm certain we can arrive at a mutually acceptable figure as to what the job is worth."

- "Salary is, of course, important to me, but it is not the most important factor. I wonder if you could tell me some of the qualifications for the job so I can get a better handle on what the compensation level should be." (This provides an opportunity to lead into your list of questions.)

- "My primary interest is in the total opportunity, rather than in salary alone. If I can ask you a question about the job, I'm certain this will be a great help."

How to Handle Questions About Employers and Accomplishments

Sometimes a PE will ask questions about your current or former employers. You should never criticize a present or past employer, even if such criticism is well deserved. For one thing, any problem in your past is a negative, even if it was not your fault. Only positive experiences and accomplishments will lead to job offers. Second, the PE may not agree with your criticism, or you may fail in some way to give all the facts. The net result could be that the PE is silently agreeing with your employer rather than with you. Finally, it may occur to your PE that if you criticize your present or past employer, you may criticize him in the future. For similar reasons, you should not betray confidences or competitive information about present or past employers.

If you are asked why you left a former employer or want to leave your present job, you must be ready with an answer. Even if you were or are about to be fired, you should work out an acceptable answer with your former employer. You do not want to give your PE one reason for leaving and have your former employer give another.

In general, you should show your expertise by the quality of your questions and your knowledge of the company, its products, and the PE. If you are asked to describe your experience and accomplishments, state them matter of factly and in quantitative terms, as you did in your sales letter. Don't say, "I increased production considerably in a short period of time." Say, "I increased production 50 percent within two months."

Body Language Can Help You Win a Job

Psychologists have discovered that we frequently reveal our innermost thoughts through visual cues provided by the body. Many salesmen have already begun to use body language in making sales by adjusting their presentation depending on what body language is telling them. You can do the same thing.

Positive Signs

Interviewer is smiling.
Interviewer is leaning forward in his chair.
Interviewer is listening attentively.
Interviewer is nodding his head affirmatively.
Interviewer's arms are unfolded.
Interviewer is looking directly at you.

Negative Signs

Interviewer is frowning.
Interviewer is drumming his fingers on the desk or noticeably playing with some object (such as pen, pencil, or article of clothing).
Interviewer is checking wristwatch periodically.
Interviewer is not making eye contact with you.
Interviewer is squirming around in his seat.
Interviewer's arms are folded in front of him.

If you are getting negative signals, you are doing something wrong. Change tactics and observe what happens.

What to Do if You Come Up Against an Expert Interviewer

On rare occasions you will come up against an expert interviewer. Such an interviewer will not put you under stress but will do everything possible to put you completely at ease and off guard. He will agree to everything you say and encourage you to say more. He will try to get you to do most of the talking. He will give you the impression that you are continually scoring points during the interview. This is the most dangerous type of interviewer to have. If you are not careful, he will get you to expose all your weaknesses, which he will coldly evaluate after the interview.

When you encounter the expert interviewer, stay calm and relaxed, but watch what you say and do not lower your guard. Do not allow yourself to be drawn into a discussion of a controversial nature, be it religion, politics, or something closer to the job. No matter how friendly or stimulating your PE, do not discuss beliefs that you know to be held by a minority of society. Do not state any strong opinions on how your PE should change his operations. If you have a unique product that would be a fine addition to your PE's line, don't discuss it until you are hired. Do not exchange any confidences.

Stay away from controversial subjects or causes or even award-winning ideas until you are safely on board with a company. You will have a much better idea of what your new company can do and what ideas can be politically sold. Your task is to sell one product, yourself. Do not make it twice as difficult by trying to sell something else at the same time.

Remember, everything you say to a PE will either boost or lower your chances of receiving a job offer. Stick to information that you know will boost your chances.

How Roy T. Lost a Job Offer Because of a Pet Belief

Roy T.'s interview went quite well until he discovered that both he and the PE were avid readers of science fiction. This common interest should have built empathy with the PE. However, Roy had a pet belief that is generally considered a bit eccentric, even though many famous people share it. Roy believed that the earth was being visited by beings from another galaxy. Roy went into some depth on this topic, and the PE appeared both interested and enthusiastic. He encouraged Roy to go on. Roy did. By the end of the interview Roy felt that he "had it made." His PE had been most friendly and agreeable. Roy never heard from the PE again.

What went wrong? True, the hiring executive was a science fiction buff;

he even thought that extraterrestial surveillance was an interesting topic and that Roy's arguments had merit. But the PE's company was a very conservative one, and interest in science fiction was limited to the executive who interviewed Roy. This executive knew that if Roy was hired he would be dealing on a daily basis with people who not only didn't read science fiction but would think of anyone with Roy's beliefs as a crackpot. The executive reasoned like this: If Roy could expose such private beliefs to a complete stranger, what might he say to his associates after joining the company? Even though the PE had a great deal of empathy with Roy, he decided not to extend an offer to someone who could disrupt his operations.

How Joe B. Lost Out Because of His Excellent Business Plan

Joe B. saw immediately the answer to his PE's problem: a perfect product that would fill in the valleys of the PE's business cycle. He launched into the presentation of a detailed business plan during the interview. What Joe didn't know was that someone else in the company had had the same idea several years before; the issue had turned into a political battle that the interviewer himself had barely survived. In fact, the interviewing executive to whom Joe so enthusiastically explained his plan was the very one who was instrumental in killing the idea. Although in many ways Joe was the ideal candidate, he didn't get an offer.

How to Gauge the Progress of the Interview

Sometimes you will get the impression that the interview is not going well and that you are going to be rejected. Conceal your feelings and continue with the interview as if nothing had happened. It may be only the personality or mood of your interviewer. Perhaps he has had a bad day or has other things on his mind. Keep your enthusiasm and positive mental attitude throughout the interview.

How can you tell whether the interview is going well? There are three definite signs, in addition to the body language cues mentioned earlier:

1. if the interviewer does more talking than you;
2. if the interviewer brings up salary or fringe benefits toward the end of the interview; and
3. if the interviewer speaks of bringing you in again to meet other members of his staff.

How to Close Out the Interview with a Sale

Never leave matters hanging at the end of the interview. If you are interested in the position, let your interviewer know it. Say something like, "I am very interested in this position. Can I expect to hear from you by Monday or Wednesday?" Or say, "The job definitely interests me. What is our next step?"

If the PE makes you an offer on the spot, do not accept immediately. Tell the PE that you are definitely interested but would like a few days to think it over. Do not say that you want to discuss it with your family, even if you do. Many PEs like to maintain the illusion that their executives are independent of their families in matters related to their careers.

If your interviewer is vague about making you an offer or about taking further action, you must regain control of the situation. Tell your PE something like this: "I want to be completely frank with you. You have a very fine company here, and I consider the position we have spoken about to be an excellent opportunity for me to do an outstanding job. However, I have another offer pending, and I must respond within the week. When will you be making me an offer?"

If you feel that you have definitely made a sale, it is time to make your salary requirements known. The PE may raise this question himself. You should be ready to use the techniques described in Chapter 20 to negotiate a significant salary increase. If you bring up the subject yourself, combine your requirements with other remarks. Tell your PE that you have another offer pending at $X and therefore would like to receive his offer as soon as possible.

The PE may delay extending you an offer because he is not fully sold on hiring you and wants to interview other candidates. If you allow the PE this chance, you could very well lose the job offer. Always remember that you are in a competitive situation. Go after and get the offer, even if you are not completely sold on the job yourself. You should be the one with several options, not your PE.

To have several offers to consider, you must aggressively go after the offer at every interview. Be smooth, polished, and dignified, but keep the pressure on your PE. Let him know that you have other offers pending.

Definite Do's

1. Be on time for the interview.
2. Dress fashionably but conservatively.
3. Be well groomed.
4. Be relaxed, enthusiastic, and friendly.

5. Be self-confident.
6. Call the interviewer by name.
7. Shake hands firmly.
8. Maintain eye contact.
9. Be a good listener.
10. Sell yourself indirectly and subtly.
11. Take notes.
12. Describe your accomplishments in quantitative terms.
13. Protect the confidence of your present or past employers.
14. If asked about your health, state that your health is excellent and do not discuss private medical problems.
15. Answer questions directly and without hesitation.
16. Get the full name and title of the executive who interviews you.
17. Prepare well before the interview.

Definite Don'ts

1. Wear frayed shirts, old clothes, bowties, mod watches, or sunglasses.
2. Smoke, unless your interviewer is smoking.
3. Chew gum.
4. Be reticent about answering questions on your experience and accomplishments.
5. Be overly aggressive or arrogant.
6. Criticize your present or past employers.
7. Apologize for any shortcomings.
8. Appear to pose a threat to your potential supervisor's position.
9. Read the mail on your interviewer's desk.
10. Look at your watch, drum your fingers, or in any other way show nervousness, boredom, or impatience.
11. Argue or allow yourself to be drawn into a discussion of controversial subjects.
12. State or imply that you can work miracles.
13. Bring in unsolicited examples of your work.
14. Inquire about salary, vacation, or other fringe benefits until you are certain that the PE is interested in hiring you.

How to Write the Interview Follow-up Letter

When you return home after the interview, take out your notes and go over them. Combine them with your preinterview notes so that you have a complete picture of your PE, the job, and the company. Fill in additional information that you think is pertinent. Do this as soon as possible after the interview, while you still have the facts in mind. You will be surprised several days later at just how little you remember. You are now ready for the next step: writing the follow-up letter.

The purpose of the follow-up letter is to remind your PE of how your experience and accomplishments are suited to his needs. You should send the letter only if you did not receive a job offer during the interview. Include a special resume if the PE has requested one. At this point, because you know the position and understand what the PE is looking for, you can tailor your qualifications precisely to the job.

The interview follow-up letter will assist you in getting the best job offer. It will convince undecided PEs that they should hire you by providing additional, documented support of your qualifications. It will also help you win out over your competitors by showing that you are the one executive who has the right experience and capabilities for the job.

You should write the follow-up letter while the facts of your interview are still fresh in your mind. Many hiring decisions are made soon after the interview, so it is to your advantage to get this additional material to the PE as quickly as possible.

The follow-up letter is constructed much like a response to an advertisement. Use the notes you made during the interview to define the requirements of the job. You may vary the format if you wish to refer to something that you discussed with the PE.

Figure 11 is a sample interview follow-up letter. Note that there is no way the writer could have prepared such a letter before the interview. He had extensive marketing experience with the federal government as well as high-level engineering management experience. However, in the letter he emphasizes his engineering experience because during the interview he discovered that his PE saw the job as a general management position that required a technical management background. In fact, the PE felt that the job did not require any functional experience in marketing.

Restating the job requirements you learned during the interview shows the PE that you understand the problem and confirms your ability to meet his requirements. Your interview follow-up letter will set you apart from other candidates seeking the job and will increase your ratio of offers to interviews. It is a must if you are serious about getting a superior job.

Figure 11. Sample interview follow-up letter.

Dear George:

Since our meeting yesterday, I have had an opportunity to review the notes I made during the interview, the requirements of the job, and my own capabilities. Seeing these laid out before me confirms what I previously felt: I can make a very smooth transition and rapid contribution to your operations in the capacity of vice president and general manager of your instrument and controls division.

It appears to me that the division's previous year's financial loss is not catastrophic and that the situation can be turned around during this fiscal year. As you indicated, you have already initiated corrective action in bidding procedures to prevent a reoccurrence of excessively low bidding. Aside from these problems, the company and current market conditions offer a number of opportunities for expansion and increased profits. It is certainly comparable to the experience you referred to when I took H&R Engineering from a $5 million loss to a $40 million profit in one year.

You have indicated to me that this division needs a forceful leader with an extensive technical background in engineering and project management of government contracts.

I am probably unique in my qualifications for this role. As program manager in NASA, I directed three successful programs in excess of $10 million, each of which came in early and under budget. Recruited into industry, I held every position from program manager through R&D director and division general manager. In total, I managed $300 million in government contracts over a five-year period.

The position of general manager is a senior one and will require considerable interaction with senior government personnel. Therefore, the job requires not only high-level technical experience but also senior contacts in government. I number among my personal friends 19 military officers of general or admiral rank and 25 civil employees of GS-15 grades or higher.

Because of the peculiar nature of government business, your new general manager must have extensive experience in preparing and bidding on responses to IFBs, RFPs, and RFQs, as well as a sound grounding in bid/no bid decision making. I have bid on government contracts and have evaluated more than 50 of them. I led the government team that evaluated the propulsion subsystem of Sea Missile and five smaller efforts. This experience assisted me a good deal in industry. As a result, I won nine of ten major programs that were bid under my direction. My batting average for programs under $100,000 is 82%.

George, I enjoyed meeting with you and am very interested in the job.

Sincerely,

John E. Smith

John E. Smith

16

How to Beat
Psychological Tests

What Psychological Tests Are and What They Measure

Psychological tests are designed to evaluate your capabilities and limitations—in short, your strengths and weaknesses. They measure, or attempt to measure, almost anything from intelligence, to sanity, to manual and mental dexterity.

Psychological testing came into wide use after World War II, reaching a peak in the late 1950s and early 1960s. There is a periodic resurgence in their use, and some companies give such tests today. Handling this particular hurdle can be just as important as other challenges you meet in your job campaign.

Why You Should Be Wary of Psychological Tests

Are psychological tests accurate? Well, they *can* be. If this is true, why not go in straight and unprepared and let the chips fall where they may? For one thing, some PEs do not always use tests properly. Even though they have had little training in administering tests or interpreting their results, they attempt to do both.

One sales firm gave all its job candidates a test and required a minimum score before extending an offer. High scorers were given preference over low scorers, regardless of a candidate's accomplishments. After several years the personnel manager became suspicious because of the turnover in sales personnel in the company. An independent consultant was hired. His analysis showed that for this company's type of selling, scores above the minimum set by the firm were excellent predictors of failure, not success. Because of the tests, the company had consistently rejected candidates who were likely to succeed.

Another reason to be wary of psychological tests is that some PEs may set unrealistically high scoring requirements. In one state the Board of Education required candidates for high school teaching positions to score in the upper 2 percent of an IQ test. Now there are only a limited number of people in this IQ group; they are not all high school teachers and do not all congregate in one state. Yet this state's school system had no trouble finding qualified teachers. How is this possible? You guessed it. Those candidates who wanted the job badly enough prepared for the test, took practice exams, and spent time working on their weak areas until they could score at the required level.

Some firms that use psychological testing in hiring give so much weight to the tests that the hiring decision is determined almost solely by the test results. But according to Dr. Irwin Rodman, a psychologist whose practice includes testing for major firms, any testing professional who is allowed to make decisions about a candidate's suitability for employment is "whistling Dixie." Dr. Rodman was quoted in the May 1982 issue of *American Business* as saying, "He's not an accountant or an engineer. He's a psychologist and he has to make clear to his corporate clientele that his technical expertise—and only his technical expertise—is what's involved." Psychological factors should never be an important consideration in a hiring decision.

Probably the best predictive test ever developed was one used to measure success in aircrew training during World War II. Almost 200,000 aviators or would-be aviators took this test, so the size of the sample population wasn't lacking. A descendant of the original test is still used today. How successful was this most successful of tests? It had a validity coefficient of .64. (A "perfect" test would have a validity coefficient of 1.0.) If you think that this doesn't sound very high, read on.

If those candidates who failed the aircraft test had been admitted into training anyway, statistics show that 56 percent would still have passed the course. Why weren't they admitted? It wasn't cost-effective to have 44 percent of a class of pilots flunk out. Further, even this most successful of tests was predicting success in training. It said nothing about success in combat. Most tests have a much lower validity coefficient than the one for aircrew selection. In fact, for the complicated skills of managers and professionals, the correlation between test scores and performance is usually less than .50.

Some people are poor test takers. For whatever reason, they consistently score lower than other executives whom they easily outperform on the job. If you have a good background and skills that are in reasonable demand, but you know that you fall short of being the world's finest test taker, your best tactic may be not to take a test at all. Tell your PE that at your level, with your accomplishments, you do not feel you should be required to take a test. If there is any doubt at all, you would be happy to furnish references to verify the information you have provided. If the PE is really interested, you will probably not be required to take a test.

How to Prepare for Psychological Testing

Preparation for any type of psychological test takes time—time you could more profitably use to get interviews. Therefore, do not go into lengthy preparations for psychological testing until you know you are going to be tested and can get some insight into what kind of test you may be given.

To prepare for psychological testing, I recommend that you take general tests offered by a university psychology department or by firms specializing in psychological testing. The latter source can be quite expensive, so if you have already had experience with such tests and have an idea how well you do, skip this phase.

If you have the chance, you should read books on psychological testing. I recommend *Psychological Testing,* by Anne Anastasi (Macmillan); *The Brain Watchers,* by Martin L. Gross (Random House); and *Theory and Practice of Psychological Testing,* by Frank S. Freeman (Holt, Rinehart and Winston). In addition, *The Organization Man,* by William H. Whyte, Jr. (Simon & Schuster), has two useful chapters—"How Good an Organization Man Are You?" and "The Tests of Conformity"—and a valuable appendix entitled "How to Cheat on Personality Tests."

How to Get Copies of Sample Tests

Copies of the following sample intelligence, personality, and interest tests are available from several sources:

Typical Intelligence Tests
Stanford-Binet, Wechsler Adult Intelligence Scale, Wonderlic Per-

sonnel Test, Otis Employment Test, Wesman Personnel Classification Test

Typical Personality Tests
California Psychological Inventory, Minnesota Multiphasic Personality Inventory, Personal Orientation Inventory, Thurstone Temperament Scale

Typical Interest Tests
Minnesota Vocational Interest Inventory, Strong Vocational Interest Blank, Occupational Interest Inventory, Kuder Occupational Interest Survey

You can obtain sample tests from friends in large personnel departments, psychological testing firms, or universities. Or you can write to companies that publish psychological tests and ask for their catalogs. Here are a few:

- American Guidance Service, Inc., Publishers' Building, Circle Pines, Minnesota 55014
- California Test Bureau, Del Monte Research Park, Monterey, California 93940
- Consulting Psychologists Press, Inc., 577 College Avenue, Palo Alto, California 94306
- Educational and Industrial Testing Service, P.O. Box 7234, San Diego, California 92107
- Houghton Mifflin Company, 1 Beacon Street, Boston, Massachusetts 02107
- Psychological Corporation, 757 Third Avenue, New York, N.Y. 10017
- Science Research Associates, Inc., 259 East Erie Street, Chicago, Illinois 60611
- E. F. Wonderlic and Associates, P.O. Box 7, Northfield, Illinois 60094

Don't spend a lot of time preparing for psychological tests until you know you have to take them. Then concentrate on the type of test you will be given and the areas in which you need to improve. For example, intelligence tests are generally divided into quantitative and verbal parts. If you are weak on the verbal side, concentrate on your vocabulary and reading ability. If you are weak on quantitative problems, concentrate on basic math, algebra, trigonometry, and geometry. The Graduate Record Examination (GRE), used by many colleges and universities, is a good general intelligence test. *How to Pass the Graduate Record Examination,* by David R. Turner (ARCO), is full of practice tests.

Two General Rules on Passing Tests

There are two general rules on how to "pass" psychological tests. First, answer personality tests as if you were an average, middle-class executive in your profession. Respond the way you think this average person would answer, not you. Don't favor any strange or radical views. Second, answer interest tests in a way that someone vitally interested in a career field would answer. That is, if you take two interest tests for a teaching position, one at College A for an English professor and the other at College B for an athletic director, your interest scales should reflect more introspective, scholarly concerns for College A and outdoorsy, leadership-type action teaching for College B.

If you are going to lie on a test, make certain that you do so consistently. Many personality and interest tests have liar scales that document your success or failure in influencing the test without drawing attention to yourself. These scales are based on a lack of consistency in answering the same question presented in several different ways. For example, the following true-false questions might be scattered throughout a single test:

- I prefer indoor activities, such as reading, to outdoor activities, such as sports.

- I spend most of my free time outdoors.

- I would prefer swimming, fishing, and walking over reading, playing chess, or listening to music.

- I would prefer boating, mountain climbing, or sunbathing over collecting stamps, doing crossword puzzles, or painting.

- My hobbies are mostly indoor activities.

A failure to answer all these questions to show a preference for either indoor or outdoor activities would affect your overall score on the liar's scale. If you answer enough sets of questions inconsistently, your score on that particular scale will suffer, as will your credibility on that particular test.

17

How to Get a Superior Job After Leaving the Service

I've devoted an entire chapter to finding a superior job after leaving the military service because I know that former military executives, especially those retiring, face unique problems in job hunting. I know this because I've been there. My father retired from the Air Force after 25 years of service and found a second career. I left the service after 11 years to pursue a special job assignment abroad.

Overcoming the First Major Problems

The first problems you will encounter are both psychological and practical. You may find that your service compensation bears little relationship to salaries on the "outside," and you have no way of knowing what you are actually worth. In addition, some PEs may feel you are overqualified for certain jobs or may not even consider your military service applicable to industry.

The key to overcoming these initial problems is to decide exactly what job you want, as discussed in Chapter 2. Learn everything you can about the job before you start your job hunt. You will need to spend much more time researching salary, position, and other matters than your civilian counterpart.

Many former military executives evaluate their job campaign totally in terms of experiences and accomplishments that brought them success in the military, rather than in terms of a specific job goal. They tell themselves: "With my background, qualifications, and education, there are any number of things I can do. Plenty of companies will immediately recognize my value and show me the options I have."

This is a mistake. It will only prolong your job campaign and reduce your chances of finding a superior job. Like your civilian counterpart, you must decide what job you want before you can go after it. This is the most important part of your campaign. Once you decide exactly what you want to do, use the techniques described below to reach your goal.

Sources of Information About Compensation in Industry

Salary requirements are an important part of any job campaign. They are particularly important if you are an ex-military job hunter because they indicate to a PE, among other things, the job level you are seeking. It is a mistake to tell a PE that salary isn't important and you are willing to work for only $X because you are already getting $Y from your military pension. Your PE will reason that you are desperate or that you don't think much of yourself.

In industry, salary has important status and other connotations. You should use salary to support the particular job level that you have decided upon. Further, in industry some power is maintained by a supervisor's ability to terminate an employee at any time. Many PEs feel insecure with subordinates who are independently wealthy or who have an outside source of income, since this lessens the power the PE has over them.

Not too long ago compensation in the military service was poor compared with compensation for positions of similar responsibility in industry. Today many military executives' salaries are very competitive with those of their civilian counterparts if items like subsistence and housing are added in. However, salary conditions vary from year to year and from industry to industry.

You can obtain salary information from a number of sources: friends in the same profession, a college or university, a search firm or employment agency, the American Management Associations (AMA) Executive Compensation Service, the personnel department of a large company in your industry, and professional organizations. It is a good idea to try all six sources of salary information so you can cross-check the figures you obtain.

Friends

Friends are a ready source of salary information, but they are also the least reliable. In fact, the information they provide can be biased, misleading, or just plain wrong. In industry, unlike the military, salary is not determined according to fixed criteria, such as rank and length of service. Further, salaries are considered confidential. It is not uncommon for executives to inflate their salaries in job hunting or to give a salary figure that includes fringe benefits.

Your friends may underestimate what you are worth in the marketplace because they do not know the value of your skills or have not had much experience with executive salaries in their industry. Unless your friends have special knowledge about executive compensation in your industry, they are probably the least reliable and desirable source of salary information.

Colleges and Universities

A college or university can be an excellent source of salary information. Your best bet is to contact the professional school in your specialty at the university you graduated from. If you don't get the information you need, try other schools. If you tell your problem to the right professor and furnish details on job title, function, and your own qualifications, chances are you will get help.

Search Firms and Employment Agencies

Many search firms and employment agencies have a specialist dealing in your function and industry. This individual may spend a good part of every day talking with PEs and job candidates in your field. Needless to say, such a recruiter has a pretty good handle on your compensation. There are limitations to this source of information, so read the chapter on headhunters before proceeding. Still, it is one of the most accurate and up-to-date sources of salary information available.

The AMA Executive Compensation Service

The American Management Associations publishes a set of annual compensation guides for most executive functions and industries. This material is intended primarily to assist companies in maintaining competitive executive compensation programs. A complete set costs more than

$1,000, but you can buy only the volume you are interested in, and some volumes cost less than $100. (You can also get a substantial discount if your company participated in the research study.) The AMA guides are excellent because they give high and low as well as average figures and are reliable and accurate.

Personnel Departments of Large Companies

Personnel departments in large companies usually maintain good compensation records and frequently have formulas for "standard" salary offers. Until you receive an offer from the company, it is rather difficult to tap this particular source, but it is worth a try. Call a personnel manager in such a company and lay your problem on the line. Explain that you are not applying for a job, but because of your long career in the military you have no idea what level of compensation you should be looking for. Find out if the personnel manager can determine a "standard" salary if you supply such information as job title, years since degree, and experience. You may encounter someone willing to run your background through a formula.

Professional Associations

Many professional associations maintain accurate salary data for your area and industry. Check your local telephone book and call. It costs nothing to ask.

How to State Your Military Accomplishments in Business Terms

The ex-military job seeker faces a major problem in that much of his military experience may be considered inapplicable to industry; at the same time, he may be considered overqualified for many civilian jobs. The military has its own system of rewards, punishments, and operating procedures. Many accomplishments that you take great pride in may be of little interest to a PE in industry. Other accomplishments that you have thought very little about may be in demand in the industrial marketplace. For example, a retired officer may prize his combat decorations and feel that he made his greatest contribution in the days when he was leading men in battle. Yet his prime attraction to a PE may be a short tour as an assistant military attaché in a foreign country, a tour for which he received only an average effectiveness report and no decorations at all.

In industry accomplishments must be related to profit—and for good reason. In a capitalist system a company must make a profit to be successful. To do this, the company must offer a better or cheaper service or product. A less efficient, less successful company will be less profitable and will be forced out of the marketplace by its competitors. The profit generated by the successful company creates additional capital for its stockholders, raising their standard of living and giving them the incentive as well as the capital to invest again. As the economy expands, new jobs are created and everyone's standard of living goes up.

Some executives coming from the military feel that the profit motive is a gross one and that industrial leaders are uniformly out to take advantage of everyone, from the common man to the U.S. government. This is absolutely wrong. Industrial leaders are no less idealistic and no more pure than leaders of ability in the military.

However, the military does not have a profit motive as such, and business and profit making are sometimes looked down upon as endeavors far afield from military concerns. Thus the military executive may view his civilian counterpart as somewhat of a rude materialist. By the same token, the civilian manager may feel that because there is no profit motive in the military, the military structure creates waste and inefficiency and military management experience is of little value to industry. The net result is that even though the former military man considers himself better qualified, better trained, and more idealistic than a civilian manager, the civilian executive may see the military man as an overqualified incompetent (as regards business management). Clearly, both attitudes are incompatible with finding a superior job in industry.

A job campaign is no place to educate anyone, and few civilian managers will try to convince you of their viewpoint or even make their viewpoint known. So in order to find a superior job in civilian life, you must bridge the military-industrial credibility gap. How do you do this? You must orient your accomplishments toward what industry is looking for, using those denominations that are common to both careers: efficiency and effectiveness.

In your sales letters, answers to advertisements, and other communications with PEs, you must make a special effort to translate your military accomplishments into terms common in the civilian marketplace. For example, translate the total amount of equipment or supplies you were responsible for into a dollar amount: "Responsible for maintaining $5 million worth of communications equipment." If you had a budget as part of your military responsibilities, mention it. Don't forget to include hidden items such as personnel salaries to arrive at the total yearly budget you were responsible for. But one word of caution about this. Those in military research and development are responsible for a much greater magnitude of dollar value than their civilian counterparts. The dollar values indicated in your sales letters should be appropriate for the job level you are seeking. A little gathering of information from people who are already in the industry you are interested in will be helpful here.

Calculate a percentage figure that reflects an accomplishment from your military experience. Describe the accomplishment in civilian rather than military terms. For example, if you are discussing an increase in reenlistments due to your efforts, you should describe it, in civilian terms, as a decrease in personnel turnover. Use quotes from your effectiveness reports to support your performance, but pick items that civilian executives can readily understand and appreciate. "Outstanding managerial ability and a first-class leader" is excellent. "Aggressive combat leader" is not, unless you're going after a soldier-of-fortune job.

How James T. Got a Superior Job
After Five Years in the Air Force

James T. was a captain with five years of service as a pilot in the Air Force. But James didn't want to fly in civilian life. He had an engineering degree and wanted to work as an aircraft designer. Here is part of the letter that James T. wrote:

> I travel at Mach 2 for a living. I would like to make it possible for other people to do the same thing more efficiently.
>
> If you are looking for an aircraft design engineer, you may be interested in other things I have done:
> - Developed a manual calculator to enable straight and level bombing by fighter aircraft during automatic equipment malfunction. Adoption of the device saved $500,000 per year in training missions.
> - Designed and built a 2-seat biplane. This plane has been granted an experimental aircraft license by the FAA and has logged over 1,000 hours under nine different pilots without an accident.
> - Graduated from special Air Force courses in electrical, hydraulic, and ordnance systems in upper 10% of my class.
> - Member of five-man team that operationally tested and improved terrain-avoidance radar. Received letter of commendation for improving mean time to failure performance by 17%.
>
> I have a BS in aeronautical engineering from the University of Illinois (1972).
>
> I would be interested in meeting with you to discuss further details in a personal interview.

This presentation meets all the requirements of the successful sales letter, the mainstay of the job campaign: opening/attention getter, explanation, motivation, credibility, and call to action.

How Douglas O. Became a Management Consultant After 28 Years in the Army

Here are parts of a letter that Douglas O. wrote after 28 years in the service. It got him an interview and ultimately a position as management consultant with a prestigious firm. I have interjected my own comments between the paragraphs. Note how Douglas translates his military accomplishments into terms that any business executive can understand.

I advised top management of a $500 million operation. Through my efforts, output was unchanged while cost was reduced by $50 million per year.

[Douglas was a staff adviser to the commander of an infantry division. Because of a major manpower cutback, he was assigned the duty of reorganizing the division according to standard Army requirements without weakening the division's ability to accomplish its wartime mission. Through imaginative thinking, Douglas succeeded. Before writing this letter, he did his own calculations and determined that the annual savings to the Army was approximately $50 million.]

If you need an experienced management consultant specializing in organization development, you may be interested in some of my other accomplishments.

[In this explanation paragraph, Douglas gives his reason for writing and specific job objective.]

As a practicing military manager, I have operational experience supervising technicians and specialists from as few as 2 to as many as 1,500. I was commended by my superiors as "an outstanding leader; a superb organizer."

[Here Douglas sums up a number of command and staff assignments during his career. The quote comes from an effectiveness report he received as commander of a battalion.]

As a staff consultant, I directed studies in 15 different organizational areas. This resulted in 101 specific recommendations for improvement. In one case, a 35% increase in efficiency resulted.

[Douglas consolidates a number of his accomplishments during a four-year tour of duty on the staff of the division commander. One study he conducted on training for physical fitness resulted in a recommendation that was adopted throughout the division. The division improved 35% on the physical fitness test.]

I have authored 73 staff studies. Of these, 51 resulted in cost savings of greater than $50,000. In 57 cases, most of the recommendations were adopted; in 12 cases, some of the recommendations were adopted. Five resulted in special awards or letters of commendation.

[Douglas sums up all the staff studies he made during his career. To do this, he reviewed copies in his file, award citations, and letters and worked out the dollar benefits in every case.]

I designed a cost control system for personnel operations that saved my employer $75,000 per year.

[Douglas describes a special assignment given to him by one of his commanders.]

I have a BS in business administration from the University of Texas, and 40 hours of work toward a master's degree in public administration from the University of Maryland and other schools.

If it is convenient, I would be able to meet with you for a personal interview sometime during the next two weeks.

How Mark K. Became a Personnel Manager After 20 Years in the Navy

Mark K. was a career naval officer who retired after 20 years of service as a lieutenant commander engaged primarily in personnel work. When he entered the Navy, Mark had no degree; during his career he went to night school and eventually graduated from City College of New York. After carefully reviewing his situation, Mark decided that he wanted to pursue a career in personnel work in a large company. Here is Mark's letter, which was addressed to the presidents or general managers of large companies:

I directed the careers of more than 2,000 executives, 31 of whom reached top management positions.

If you are in need of a corporate director of personnel, you may be interested in the following information on my background:

- Created a career development program for 500 selected executives in the U.S. Navy. Effort was termed "a program for our best people" by the Chief of Naval Operations and was described by immediate supervisors as "unique and outstanding."
- Maintained detailed personnel records of 10,000 employees from the most junior to top management. Commended for "a difficult job well done."
- Directed affirmative action programs that placed 25 senior minority executives in upper middle management and top management jobs.
- Developed manpower policies that decreased personnel turnover by 17%.

- Directed development of selection criteria for attendance of middle managers at technical and professional schools. To date, they have been used in the selection of more than 10,000 attendees.

I have a BA in business administration, specializing in personnel management, from the City College of New York.

I am looking forward to meeting you and am prepared to discuss additional details of my experience in a personal interview.

How to Emphasize Your Accomplishments and De-emphasize Your Military Experience

Note how the writers of all these letters de-emphasize their military experience, stating their accomplishments as much as possible in business terms. This does not mean that you should keep your military background a secret. However, you should not emphasize it, nor should you state in your sales letter that all your experience was obtained in the military.

Much of your military experience can be extremely valuable to an industrial PE. Unfortunately, many civilian PEs do not appreciate military experience per se. If you emphasize your military experience or indicate that all your experience has been in the military, you will have a much lower letter-to-interview ratio than your civilian counterpart.

If you present your experience in terms that the PE can understand, you will be invited in for more interviews and will get a superior job much quicker, even if you tell your PE during the interview that you obtained all your experience in the service. Remember, in job hunting you are not obligated to volunteer information when it is not in your interest to do so. If you are asked over the phone about the companies you have worked for, put off your answer until the interview.

Should You Reveal Your Military Rank?

Normally, you should not state your military rank in your sales letter or volunteer your military rank during an interview. However, you can do so if you achieved a very high rank, or a high rank relative to the number of years served, or if military rank is of some importance to your PE. In short, state your military rank only if it appears as an advantage to your PE. If it is not, do not volunteer the information under any circumstances. State it only if specifically asked.

In order to find a superior job in industry in the shortest possible time, you must overcome the initial hurdles by defining the exact civilian job goal you want. Use all the techniques described in this chapter to gain accurate salary information. Always state your military accomplishments in business terms (dollars, percentages). De-emphasize your military background and quote your effectiveness reports from the service in your sales letters and other communications.

To find a superior job, you must get high-quality, face-to-face interviews. Be evasive if necessary, and do not volunteer information that will hurt your chances for an interview.

18

How to Make the Personnel Manager an Ally Instead of an Adversary

Why Your Interests and Those of the Personnel Manager May Not Coincide

You will discover very early in your job campaign that your interests and objectives do not coincide with those of the personnel manager. The reason is simple. The personnel manager works for the company and represents the PE's interests. It is his responsibility to screen job candidates and recommend only those he feels are well qualified. Obviously, the screening process is usually highly subjective. Many a manager rejected by personnel has found a way to go around the personnel manager, get the job anyway, and become highly successful.

The personnel manager can be an obstacle between you and an offer of employment. For most executive positions, the personnel manager does not make the decision to hire, but he may have the authority to stop you from seeing the hiring executive. This amounts to the authority not to hire you. For this reason, you should avoid contact with the personnel manager (except to obtain intelligence about the job) until the PE has made you an offer. Your job campaign should always be focused on the hiring executive, not the personnel manager.

How to Make Use of the Personnel Manager

Sometimes contact with personnel managers is unavoidable. When this happens, it is imperative to turn the situation around so that a liability becomes an asset. For example, hiring executives may have personnel managers contact you rather than doing so themselves. You should immediately take advantage of this opportunity by obtaining as much information about the job as possible.

Sometimes a PE will send you an employment form. As I have noted elsewhere in this book, unless you know that you are being considered for a specific job, it is generally a waste of time to complete employment forms. If you receive such a form, call the individual who sent it to you (usually the personnel manager) and try to determine if a specific opening exists. If you are told that you must complete the form first, don't waste your time filling it out.

No matter what happens, never be arrogant or discourteous to a personnel manager. He may not be a real help in getting you a job offer, but he can be a hindrance. Also, even if there are no current openings for which you qualify, an opening may come up within a few weeks.

If a PE gives you a choice between sending a resume or completing an employment form, choose the resume, since you can more easily shape it to the image you want to project.

Sometimes you will be asked to meet with the personnel manager before seeing the hiring executive. If you are given an employment form to complete at this time, do not fill it out. Always ask to be allowed to complete the form at home, where you have all the information available.

If you fill out an employment form on the PE's premises, you will be rushed and may not get everything down the way you want to. Also, the information you supply on such a form tends to become frozen exactly as written. If you must fill one out, you need time to word the information carefully. After the interview, you will know a great deal more about the job and will be able to slant your experience and background to it.

What You Should Not Discuss with the Personnel Manager

Whenever you talk with personnel managers, try to get as much information as you can about the job while minimizing what you reveal about yourself. For example, if you have called in response to an advertisement and are asked for specifics about your background, try to ask some questions first. Find out all you can about the qualifications for the job. If you are pressed for details, say that you meet all the qualifications stated in the advertisement but prefer not to go into specifics until you know more, since you do not want to take the chance of losing your present job. In general, the less you say the better, even after you have learned the requirements of the position and can orient your accomplishments to these requirements.

Remember, the personnel manager cannot help you, only hurt you. If you are calling to get information, you need not reveal even your name. Regardless of what happens, you will lose nothing, since you are going to reach the hiring executive in some other manner. However, if you are contacting the personnel manager because you have been directed to do so by a PE, you will have to reveal information about your background. In this case, you must use your judgment on what to reveal as well as how far to push the personnel manager for information before you say anything about yourself.

How to Use the Personnel Manager for Debriefings

Personnel managers are a good source for debriefing after an interview with the hiring executive, especially if you did not receive a job offer. If you have met the personnel manager before your interview with the hiring executive, call or visit him immediately afterward. Tell him that you enjoyed the interview and give him some positive feedback on what happened. Do not tell the personnel manager anything told to you in confidence. Do tell him where you left matters with the PE: "She's going to let me know on Wednesday" or "I'll be back to meet the president on Friday." Then if the hiring executive doesn't follow through, you have someone else to contact and query.

Maintain a sense of urgency by telling the personnel manager about a previous offer: "I sure hope Bob doesn't delay if he intends to make an offer. I have an offer pending already, and I must respond by Friday." If the personnel manager is friendly toward you, he may take it upon himself to remind the hiring executive to make a decision about you soon.

When an interview does not result in an offer, debriefing is essential. Once you are certain that an offer will not be extended, try to find out why from both the hiring executive and the personnel manager. Tell the personnel manager that you would appreciate his frankness, since any failing or blemish in your background could cost you another job in the future.

If the personnel manager hesitates or says that you were great, only someone else was better, tell him that you know you aren't perfect, no one is, and ask for your weak points as it pertained to this job. Never be defensive, volunteer a shortcoming, attempt to explain a fault, or be argumentative, even if what the personnel manager tells you is inaccurate. Always thank the personnel manager for the critique. Take good notes, and don't repeat the same mistake twice.

When to Call the Personnel Manager and When to Call the Hiring Executive

There are times when it is better to call the personnel manager, times when it is better to call the hiring executive, and times when it is better to call both.

In the preinterview stage, when you are gathering information about the job, you should talk to both the personnel manager and the hiring executive. Often when a hiring executive receives your sales letter, he will ask you to call the personnel manager or even have the personnel manager call you himself. In that case, the decision has been made for you. In some companies the personnel manager may withdraw from the picture after an interview has been set up. In other companies he will continue to participate in the hiring process. You may be directed to come by the personnel office before your interview with the hiring executive.

After the interview, if you have already met the personnel manager, stop by his office and bring him up to date, as suggested previously. Obviously, you should *not* do this (unless directed to by the hiring executive) if the PE told you he was handling everything from here on or if you did not get along with the personnel manager.

If you have a postinterview question, it is generally better to ask the hiring executive. However, you can use the question as a reason to get back to the personnel manager and find out how the interview went. If you are on good terms with the personnel manager, you can also use him as a "how goes it" to keep track of the offer as it develops. Be sensitive to everything you say and hear about the job and the hiring process. And remember that the desires of the hiring executive always take precedence over those of the personnel manager.

How to Use the Personnel Manager During Salary Negotiations

Personnel managers can be useful during salary negotiations. This is especially true in large companies, where personnel managers may have considerable influence over the salary range. For example, if you want to know how high the hiring executive can go, you could call the personnel manager and tell him that you have a tentative offer of $X, a figure 10 percent higher than the offer from his company. Casually ask whether the personnel manager thinks that the hiring executive can meet this offer. You may get some important information. A particularly friendly personnel manager may even suggest that he let the hiring executive know that you would accept the offer for another 10 percent.

What to Do During a Screening Interview
with the Personnel Manager

If you have a screening interview with a personnel manager, put everything into the interview, just as if it were with the hiring executive. Use every technique described in Chapter 15. If you have competitors, try to find out about them. You may learn something from the personnel manager that will help you beat the competition.

For example, during a screening interview with the personnel manager Louise S. learned that her leading competitor had no production experience, a fact that bothered the hiring executive. During her interview Louise found a way to stress her own production experience and to mention that she felt it was a prerequisite for the job. It is impossible to say whether Louise got the job for this reason. But what she said could only strengthen the hiring executive's conviction that the other candidate did not have adequate experience.

The personnel manager can be of assistance in your campaign if you use him instead of allowing him to use you. To do this, you must be careful about everything you say to both the hiring executive and the personnel manager. Practice the techniques discussed in this chapter and you will be able to use every contact with personnel to your advantage.

19

How to Insure That You Have Superior Reference Checks

Why Companies Make Reference Checks

Most companies use reference checks as one means of verifying your background. Usually, such checks are made after a job offer is extended, or at least after you have become a serious candidate for the job. Sometimes an offer is made contingent on your references "checking out." In this case, the reference check is the final hurdle. It can eliminate otherwise well-qualified candidates or cause them to lose out to competitors with better references.

Frequently checks are made not only on those people you supply as references (the PE assumes that these will be good, or why would you have given them?) but also on former supervisors, associates, and even subordinates. Keep in mind that the PE can contact anyone who may be able to comment on your work experience, character, or ability.

More frequently than you might think, job hunters get poor recommendations from supposedly excellent references. Executive recruiters discover this all the time in checking references supplied by their candidates. Here are examples from the files of headhunters.

How Dan G. Got a Bad Reference
from His Former Roommate

Dan G., a brilliant young physicist, had received his Ph.D. with honors and spent eight years with one firm. He gained an excellent professional reputation and was promoted well ahead of his contemporaries. When Dan was recruited by a headhunter for a position as manager of research and development, he listed his roommate from his graduate days in college as a personal reference.

All Dan's references checked out; in fact, they were outstanding. That is, all but one. Dan's former roommate said the following: "Dan is a nice fellow, but not very reliable. I guess you knew it took him five years to get his bachelor's degree. Also, I've heard that he was moved up too fast in his present company, and I'm certain that's going to block any future promotions for him. I guess he'd be O.K. as a manager as long as he were closely supervised."

How Mort T. Got a Bad Reference
After Saving His Company

Mort T. was a general manager who saved several companies from bankruptcy and made them profitable. He was acclaimed in his field by customers, competitors, and associates alike. In his next-to-last job, as president reporting to a chief executive officer, he had pulled a company out of the red, more than doubled sales, and built more organizational élan than any manager before or since. Here's what Mort's former boss said when contacted by a headhunter: "Mort was an outstanding leader, but he was very stubborn and would never take advice. He did a good to excellent job but couldn't seem to get along with anyone. I really can't recommend him."

Because of this unexpected response, the headhunter called other executives at the company to ask about Mort. The first corporate officer at Mort's level said, "Mort is a superior manager, a very gifted guy who turned the company around." The financial executive at Mort's old company commented, "Mort really knows his stuff. He has the knack of knowing exactly what to do to get everyone pulling in the same direction." Finally, Mort's replacement, his former deputy, told the headhunter, "A very hard act to follow. Mort did things for this company that I don't think anyone else could have done. He had everybody working overtime and actually loving it."

Why Job Hunters Are Given Bad References

There are dozens of stories of executives whose references did not check out, although by logic and reason they should have. Can you imagine what might have happened had any of the above references been the only one who could be reached? Or what if the job hunter was really unlucky and two of his references failed to check out? What would be the results if the competition between two job candidates was particularly close?

Why are job hunters like Dan and Mort given unfair references?

The motivation can be jealousy. Dan's former roommate was also a physicist. Dan had forged ahead and was ready to take over major responsibilities as an R&D manager. Dan's friend was still at square one. Mort's former supervisor resented Mort's accomplishments and saw him as a threat to his own position. In fact he was half afraid that the headhunter was recruiting Mort for his very job. Mort's superior performance made it impossible for the corporate officer to fire him, but this did not prevent him from giving Mort a bad reference.

The Secret of Always Giving Superior References

What can you do to prevent your references from unexpectedly turning sour? First, prepare your references before they are contacted. If you are not conducting a campaign in secret, talk to each potential reference, including former employers. Tell each your job objective and explain what you would like the reference to say. Don't be bashful. If you did a great job for some people and you'd like them to emphasize it, tell them. This preparation is especially important with a former employer, since you must establish an agreed-on and acceptable reason for leaving your job.

Second, try to locate any hidden bombs before they go off. Have every reference checked out. The best way to do this is to have a friend check them for you. Make up a list of at least ten questions that a PE or headhunter might ask: "Under what circumstances do you know the candidate?" "What kind of person is she?" "Is he reliable?" "Is he suited to management?" Review these questions with your reference checker and make certain that he sounds professional. Your checker's dialogue might go something like this: "Hello, Mrs. Smith? This is Clark Baker of Worldwide Search. One of your former employees, Jim Jones, is being considered for a senior financial position with one of my clients. I wonder if I could take a few minutes of your time for a reference check?"

No matter what happens, your checker must not admit that he is anything except what he says he is. If he is asked questions about the job, company, or industry, he should say that he is not permitted to divulge this information.

If you discover a bad reference, don't use it. If the reference is a personal or professional one, just substitute a good reference. What can you do if the reference is a former supervisor? Well, if you don't name the former company, your former supervisor won't be contacted. If the PE insists that you name former companies, you can give the names and numbers of good references at each company and leave out your former supervisor. If you locate only one bad reference among former supervisors, try to find out the reason for it. Tell your PE about it and offer him good references at the same company.

What to Do After Your References Have Been Verified

Once you have completed your checking, make a list of dependable personal, professional, and former employer references. Always make sure that these references are not called until you are definitely interested in a job offered by a PE and the PE is definitely interested in you. If you do not protect your references, along about check number ten your references are going to become somewhat less than enthusiastic about you. Protect your references by adopting the policy that "references will be furnished only if there is mutual interest." If your references are senior, give your PE a hint by listing titles only. "U.S. senator," "president of a medium-size manufacturing company," and "professor of management" are impressive without giving away a thing.

The reference check is one of the final obstacles between you and a superior job. If you neglect to check out references yourself, that critical commitment by your PE, the job offer, may never be made.

20

How to Negotiate a Significant Salary Increase

How to Negotiate in the Prenegotiation Stage

The prenegotiation stage is the period before you have made a sale. Up to this point you have deferred all talk of compensation. But the interview is going well and it is time to approach the subject. Your objective is to give salary guidance to your PE while avoiding direct questions or discussions of salary.

The best approach is an indirect one. For example, you can describe an experience you had with your company car. This will alert the PE to the fact that you expect a company car or equal compensation. Or you can tell a story about a subordinate and mention his salary. The salary level you assign to your subordinate will give the PE an idea of what salary you expect. Say anything you want in the way of a subtle hint, but do not come out and state your compensation requirements.

The key to success in the interview, or in any dialogue with the PE, is to listen. By listening carefully you will know when you are about to get an offer. The PE will begin to sell the job to you. He will describe the advantages of the job, the company, working conditions, or recreational opportunities. The crucial moment is when the PE begins to describe fringe benefits. This is one reason that you should not bring up fringe benefits yourself. If you allow your PE to do it, you will know that you have made a sale and will gain a psychological advantage in negotiation.

How to Avoid Negotiating from Your Old Salary

In many human endeavors there are guiding principles of success that must be observed. In salary negotiations there is such a principle. It can be stated simply: *If you are trying to negotiate a significant increase in salary, do not make your present or previous salary the basis of negotiations.*

If you are already making a satisfactory salary, you may be seeking a superior job for another reason—for example, to improve your opportunity for advancement or to get out of an impossible political situation. In this case, you may want to reveal your previous salary and negotiate from there.

If you are after a significant salary increase, there is an important fact that you must know. Most American companies will try to use your previous salary as a starting point for negotiations and will try to limit increases to 10 to 15 percent of your previous salary. Yes, even though this policy is obviously shortsighted, the average PE wants to get a bargain. A bargain to him is as close to your previous salary as possible, assuming your previous salary is not high and he has no other guidelines.

To avoid negotiating from your old salary, you must give your PE some other basis for negotiations. One good basis is what the job is actually worth to other companies. Before going into the interview, you should obtain accurate salary information about the job, taking into account industry, function, title, geographical location, and size of company. As discussed in Chapter 17, you can obtain this information from friends, headhunters, the AMA's compensation service, and colleges or universities. Sometimes professional societies can help you out. Try to get a good idea of exactly what you are worth so you do not inadvertently price yourself out of the market and so you can speak with authority when discussing salary with a PE. Prepare your research carefully before you begin overt negotiations.

You have been alerted that an offer is about to be made. Now the PE will probably ask you, "What is your present salary level?" or "How much were they paying you at the XYZ Company?" or perhaps "What compensation do you require?" You should preface your answer by telling the PE that you researched compensation for the job, size of company, and geographical area before the interview. Then your pitch might go like this: "The Engineers Association 1983 Survey shows a salary range from

$35,000 to $43,000 per year, with a median figure of $40,000 per year. I believe I am exceptional, or you wouldn't want to hire me in the first place. Therefore, I think that $X to $Y is a fair range. Agreed?" The X and Y, of course, are top and bottom of the salary range you have decided on.

Another basis for negotiation available to every job hunter is the mythical offer. It can be used either by itself or in conjunction with your researched salary figures. If a PE asks you your present salary or desired compensation, say, "Well, I already have an offer at $X." If the PE balks at the range determined by your research, you can come through with the statement about your salary research. As long as you haven't priced yourself out of the market, the PE will begin to negotiate with you.

Why You Should Not Lie About Your Present Salary

Sometimes I am asked the obvious question: Why not lie about your present salary—make it much higher than it actually is—and negotiate from there? I do not recommend this. Aside from any ethical considerations, it is easy for a PE to find out your actual salary if he wants to. A surprisingly large number of companies will release this information to anyone who claims to have a need to know. Some "friends" from former companies will gleefully give a formal denial when asked to confirm the figure you have stated to your PE. Or the PE could ask you to produce a W-2 withholding form or even your federal income tax return. Then, of course, there are agencies that specialize in background checks. Ergo, lying is not recommended.

If for some reason you are forced into revealing your current salary, there are acceptable tactics you can use to enhance the picture. You can give a figure that includes an expected salary increase. For example, if your annual raises have been averaging 10 percent over the last few years, you can add that expected 10 percent. Or you can include the dollar value of fringe benefits such as bonus, car, and stock options.

Why You Shouldn't Give a Single Figure During Negotiations

Negotiations require a good deal of "indirection" and patience. After the strain of a vigorous job campaign and the stress of the interview, many job hunters feel great relief and goodwill knowing that they are about to get an offer. As a result, they want to be direct and have done with it. "Look," they would like to tell the PE, "I know you want me, and you know I would like to come to work for you. I need $X per year in order to do this."

Such directness is generally a mistake. Even if you really have only one salary figure in mind, do not say so. If you do, you surrender all psychological advantages to the PE. Any additional negotiating—for example, moving expenses and other conditions of employment—will rest in the PE's favor, not yours, even if he agrees to your salary figure. Many PEs enjoy negotiating and may not be as eager as you to conclude the deal. If you cite a single salary figure, the PE will start to negotiate from there—and I promise you that the bargaining process is always downward, never upward.

More than likely, your salary goal consists of two figures: the top a figure you feel you can achieve, the bottom a minimum you would accept. It is always best to give the range in negotiations. If you state only the high figure, the PE may feel he cannot get you at a lesser figure. If he can meet your demand, that's fine. If he cannot, or has a lower figure in mind, you may find it difficult to reestablish negotiations. If you state the lower figure, you may lose money because the PE was ready to pay more, or the PE may have second thoughts about hiring you because you have asked for less than he felt the job was worth. By citing a range of compensation—and giving it some credibility by mentioning a respected source for your information—you protect yourself, enhance your negotiating position, and allow negotiations to continue regardless of what the PE has in mind.

What to Do When the PE Counters Your Salary Range

Let's review where we are. During prenegotiations you gave some broad hints about salary without giving an exact figure or mentioning salary directly. During the interview, when you realized that you had made a sale, you stated a specific salary range to negotiate from. Several things can happen at this point:

- The PE may name a salary figure within your range that you find acceptable.
- The PE may counter with a salary at the lower end of your range (or below it) that you find unacceptable.
- The PE may state his own salary range, which may or may not overlap yours.
- Finally, the PE may defer a decision, stating that he must discuss the matter with his staff and asking you to return for a second interview.

If the PE names an acceptable salary, you can either stop negotiating or continue to negotiate for more. You could, for example, tell the PE that you feel the job is worth $X (a figure 5 percent higher than the PE's offer). The decision to continue negotiating calls for careful judgment, and only you, on the spot, can make it. However, you should know that few PEs will eliminate you because you asked for 5 percent more, and you should keep in mind that an annual salary increase may be no more than 5 percent.

If the PE counters with a range, your target is of course the upper part of that range. Chances are you will not be able to get more than the top figure. However, if your minimum acceptable salary is above this, now is the time to say so. Tell the PE that the job appears very challenging and you feel you would enjoy working for the company; however, you already have an offer for $X (a figure 10 to 20 percent higher than your minimum acceptable figure) and feel the minimum acceptable salary taking all factors into consideration is $Y (a figure X percent above your minimum). You will leave room for further negotiations without going below your minimum acceptable figure, and you may still get more than your minimum amount.

If the PE refuses to move into your acceptable range, thank him for his offer and tell him you are unable to accept. Let him know that you are still very interested in the job, and ask him to contact you in the next week or so if there is any way that the salary level can be increased. If the PE says that it is impossible to go higher, try to make up the difference by negotiating for fringe benefits above the standard package offered.

In addition to salary, you can try negotiating for a company automobile, an expense account, club memberships, a bonus, or stock options. You might also consider more frequent salary reviews or an initial review after three to six months. Sometimes even though the PE cannot increase the basic salary for the job, he can increase the fringe benefits, so this approach is more than worthwhile.

If an impasse occurs, tell the PE that you'd like a few days to think the situation over. Using the techniques described earlier in the book, make an appointment for an additional interview on the spot. Before you return for the second round, think up several additional arguments to support your minimum acceptable figure. If the PE appears uninterested at this point, or if you sense that he will not change his stated (unacceptable) offer and will not or cannot negotiate fringe benefits, it is best to thank him, break off negotiations, and not waste any more of your time.

What if the top figure of the PE's range is within your range? The situation is similar to that of the single-figure offer, except that you now have a top figure to which the PE may be willing to go. Obviously this top figure is your target, even if it exceeds your salary goal. One way of going after the top figure is to cite your mythical offer. Tell the PE that you already have an offer at $X (the PE's top figure). In response, the PE may meet or even better the mythical offer. At worst, he will probably continue negotiating.

What to Do After You Get the Offer

Once you and the PE agree on an acceptable figure, you should confirm the offer: "Let me see if I understand the offer correctly. Annual salary will be at $X with the following fringe benefits. . . ." Write it all down in your notebook. Tell the PE you would like a couple of days to consider the offer and will let him know by a specific date. This will allow you to conclude the interview with an offer in your pocket. A PE will rarely withdraw an offer, and in the interval you can reconsider all aspects of the job and wait for additional offers to mature.

Many PEs prefer not to make an offer on the spot. Others may delay so that they can consider additional candidates. If your PE does not make an offer during the interview, remind the PE of your mythical offer at $X. Ask him to contact you by a specific day within a week. If you do not retain control over the hiring situation, you may find yourself on a string until the PE finds someone else. You must not allow this to happen. Maintain a sense of urgency by letting the PE know that he is in competition for your services and must act quickly.

If you are unemployed, such a positive mental attitude is especially valuable. Clearly, your negotiating position would be stronger if you were employed and not dependent on finding a job. However, you can make your negotiating position appear just as strong or stronger by convincing the PE that you have another offer at a competitive salary.

If salary discussions are postponed and you receive an offer by phone, use the techniques described earlier in this chapter to conclude negotiations. You may also receive an offer by mail. If it isn't satisfactory, you can open negotiations by calling and asking for another interview; should distance make this impossible, you can negotiate by telephone.

How to Negotiate with Several PEs Simultaneously

If you have several offers going at the same time, you are in an ideal position. Don't hesitate to play one PE against the other, as long as you maintain your dignity, do not become arrogant, and do not actually accept an offer. Once you accept an offer, you should shut off all negotiations.

Sometimes after a job candidate has accepted one offer, another PE will counter with an offer that is significantly higher. The lesson here is that there is a lot of room for negotiation before accepting a salary offer. For example, Larry L. had a successful interview and was told he would receive an offer by mail. Larry understood that the offer would be approximately $40,000 a year—this was, in fact, Larry's salary goal. The next day Larry had an interview with another firm and received an on-the-spot offer of $40,000.

After thinking things through, Larry decided to accept the second offer, since it met his salary objective and offered other advantages. In the meantime he received an offer from the first PE in the mail, also at $40,000. Larry called the second PE and accepted that offer. He then called the first PE to let him know. The PE immediately countered by offering $45,000.

If you accept one offer and afterward receive a significantly better deal from someone else, be completely frank with both PEs. If one offer is really that much better, few PEs will stand in your way; but if you have accepted the offer already, the option should be theirs. Tell the PE who has made the "significantly better" offer that your acceptance (if that is your decision) is contingent on being released from your previous obligation.

Where the Higher Salaries Are

As a rule, larger companies can afford to pay the highest salaries. However, such companies may be more rigid than smaller firms in negotiating salary and fringe benefits. Smaller companies may offer very competitive salaries when they need a candidate's services immediately. Salary policies can vary widely, so never take a paticularly low salary offer as a personal insult or as a final figure. Try to negotiate an acceptable figure; if you can't, move on.

To negotiate the highest salary possible, always be pleasant and courteous and maintain a positive mental attitude. If you research salary carefully and use the other techniques described in this chapter, you will be able to negotiate a superior salary in line with your superior job.

Job Counseling Services:
When and How
to Use Them

Why You May Not Want to Use Executive Job Counselors

Many job-finding books and articles in business magazines have expressed negative attitudes toward job counseling for executives. A friend and executive recruiter who heads his own successful executive search firm, and with whom I have given a number of job-finding seminars, expresses the idea most succinctly: "There is nothing that an executive job counselor can do for you that you cannot do for yourself better and with less expense." If you apply the techniques in this book, you can do a better job than anyone else could possibly do for you under most circumstances. This is because you know the product (yourself) better than anyone else; you can control the pace of your own campaign, and no one will fight as hard for you as you will fight for yourself.

Another argument against using executive job counselors is that partial counseling services are available for a fraction of the cost. For example, the University of California at Los Angeles has a career counseling center that caters both to executives and to students. This center's program includes the following:

PRELIMINARY INTERVIEWS

You discuss with your counselor—a psychologist—your specific career problem, your education, your work experience to date, and other facts in your background which could relate to your choice of a career goal.

TESTING

You take tests carefully selected to meet your individual situation and your interests, abilities, special aptitudes, and personality needs. You do not pass or fail these tests. The results help you and your counselor study your preferences, needs, strengths, and weaknesses. Your test results are professionally analyzed by psychologists trained in individualized test interpretation and aware that tests can have widely varying implications for different individuals.

EVALUATION INTERVIEWS

Test results are integrated with background data and are fully discussed by you and your counselor to help you understand yourself and your potential for personal, career, and/or educational growth. You discuss with the counselor the various careers suggested as appropriate for you and formulate plans for reaching your chosen objective.

Where educational or training plans are involved, you discuss appropriate colleges and majors, or other schools, training facilities, or individual courses.

WRITTEN SUMMARY

A summary including test results and counseling conclusions is mailed to you after the program has been completed.

The charge for this entire program is currently $425—perhaps one-tenth of the cost of using an executive job counselor. For many executives, such partial counseling services are a better investment.

A final drawback of using executive job counselors is that none of them can guarantee you any job. But I believe that you *can* guarantee yourself a job—and a superior one—by knowing the correct techniques and then applying them.

How Executive Counseling Can Help You

Despite these disadvantages, my own investigation did uncover a number of reasons why it may be in your interest to use an executive job counselor. Here are some:

1. *These services can save you time.* Many executive job counselors have the resources to put an entire campaign together—and the people to put it together rapidly. Robert Jameson Associates advertises in its brochure, "We can provide you with the latest search techniques, identify your career options, plan your search, write your resumes and letters, recommend employers to contact, and supply newly released job openings from throughout the nation. We can also handle your printing and typing, market you, and guide you throughout all interviews. In short, we can work with you wherever you need help."

Clearly, what this firm is offering to do encompasses much of what I have described in this book. Since the firm apparently has the resources to accomplish this, it could save you a lot of time.

2. *You get counseling from other executives.* Many successful executive job hunters need no one to counsel them besides immediate family and friends. Others benefit from job counseling with psychologists, like those at the UCLA Counseling Center I spoke of previously. However, many executives prefer counseling from other executives on a professional basis. They are not comfortable discussing the intimate details of their own careers, problems, frustrations, opportunities, and so forth with executive friends. But they do feel a need to discuss these things with someone who knows the score. In these cases executive job counselors are ideal since most have been in the front-line trenches themselves. Such counseling can often continue throughout the job campaign, including the negotiation of the offer once it is made. Clearly, this is a much more job-focused type of counseling than can be provided by a university psychologist.

3. *These firms can make additional job-finding services available to you.* Some services may not be available at home. You may or may not have your own videotape machine. Even if you have one and your family or friends are willing to spend the time with you to videotape a role-playing interview and then help to critique your performance, this is bound to be a somewhat amateurish affair. You'll pay for such services with an executive job consultant, but you can usually count on a professional job and critique. If it helps you win the interview that you wouldn't otherwise win, it may be worth the money.

4. *Many executives are accustomed to delegating specialized tasks that they cannot do for themselves.* An executive is unlikely to write his own computer program unless that is his specialty, and even then if he is a manager he will probably have someone else do this for him. The same can be said in other cases. A marketing manager may not do her own marketing research; an engineering manager is unlikely to do his own detail design. Because executives are accustomed to delegation, many executives feel more at ease delegating the majority of tasks in job finding

rather than handling them themselves. Such executives, if they have the money, probably should not fight the problem. They should do the maximum that they feel comfortable with themselves and should probably delegate the rest to an executive job counselor.

5. *An executive job counselor is, in many senses, a teacher who can help to motivate you.* Throughout your job campaign it is inevitable that you will have ups and downs in motivation, times when your morale will be higher and times when it will be lower. A good executive counselor can act as a teacher and motivate you to greater accomplishment under all circumstances. It is very difficult for a spouse or a friend to fulfill this function the way a professional can.

How to Screen a Job Counseling Firm

If you are thinking about using an executive job counselor, I want to caution you in two areas. First, beware of some very sophisticated marketing techniques that are used. If you contact a job counseling firm either through the mail or by telephone, you can expect efforts to persuade you to visit the counselor for a "no charge" interview. You can also expect that during this interview, the firm will sell you on its services and may apply considerable pressure for you to sign up for its program. Finally, you may expect that these services will not come cheap. At a minimum you will be paying several thousand dollars. The unfortunate thing about the strong sales tactics is that they come at a time when the executive job hunter may be desperate. It is hard to make a clear-headed decision for or against employing the counselor under such circumstances. Therefore, you should avoid signing any contract for services with an executive career consultant or counselor without a thorough investigation. This investigation should take the following form:

1. *Ask for the names of five executives that you can talk to who have used this firm's services.* Naturally, you can expect all these executives to be boosters of the firm under question. But you should have your own list of questions when you talk to these executives. Sometimes, even though the response is favorable, you will uncover facts that make it clear that this specific firm is not for you.

2. *You should not be embarrassed at all to ask what the success rate has been in helping executives.* Most firms will clearly state that they cannot guarantee a job for you. However, you want to know how many people actually found their jobs as a result of using their services. Now, it is easy to lie here, and you may not get a forthright answer. But merely asking the question gives you an opportunity to observe how the person

answers it—or evades it—and you will learn a lot about how he conducts his business.

3. *Insure that you get in writing exactly what the executive job counselor is going to do for you in return for the money you are going to pay.* I emphasize here that this should be in writing. Don't confuse vague promises with what you think you are contracting for. If something that has been promised verbally is not in the contract, have it written into the contract or don't sign the contract.

4. *Check with the Better Business Bureau in your area.* One or two complaints may mean nothing. On the other hand, a number of negative reports definitely indicate that there is a problem. In any case, if there is some question, you should feel no embarrassment about asking representatives of the firm to explain the situation themselves.

5. *Finally, you should check around on your own.* Ask friends not only whether they have used the services but whether they know or have heard of anyone else who has. Remember that any type of consulting is a very personal thing. Therefore, even a well-known firm that may be great in one city may not do as well in another city; or even within a firm, certain counselors will do a better job than others. Therefore, the more you can find out about them on an individual basis, the better off you will be.

6. *Find out whether the person actually speaking to you is the one that will be performing the services.* You want to deal with someone you feel comfortable with. However, sometimes you will find that the counselor you are talking with does only the selling. You will be turned over to someone you haven't met before once you are on contract.

To sum up, I think that you must weigh the advantages and disadvantages clearly before you sign a contract with an executive job counselor. However, if your situation requires such services and you thoroughly investigate the firm and what it has to offer, an executive job counselor can be of help. Just be certain you know what you are getting and exactly what it will cost.

22

Successful
Executive Job Campaigns

Since the publication of the first edition of *The Executive's Guide to Finding a Superior Job,* I have heard from executives across the country who have used the guide successfully. In this chapter I will present just a sampling of the stories of those I've heard from: their campaigns and the results they achieved.

From Engineering Manager to General Manager

E.C. had been a NASA manager for 20 years. He sought to use in industry the skills he had used in government, so he went to work for a major aerospace company as an engineering manager at a good salary. However, E.C. soon discovered that the scope of his responsibilities was much below his capabilities and his desires for a career outside of government. He obtained a copy of *The Executive's Guide to Finding a Superior Job* and initiated a campaign after first deciding exactly what he was looking for. E.C. wanted to remain in the same geographical area but to have total engineering responsibilities for a company. This implied responsibilities as either a director or vice president of engineering.

E.C.'s campaign involved sending sales letters, answering advertisements both through a targeted letter alone and in combination with use of the telephone, contacting search firms, and using personal contacts.

Because he was employed at the time, his campaign was conducted in secret.

Being a careful engineer, E.C. kept precise records of both the input to and the output from his campaign. These were as follows:

Sales letters sent, 196
Ads answered, 25
Search firms contacted, 15
Personal contacts, 8
Total inquiries, 244

That was the input. The output was as follows:

Sales letters resulted in 4 interviews and 2 offers. Written responses to ads by themselves resulted in 2 interviews with 0 offers.
Phone responses to advertisements combined with written responses resulted in 2 interviews with 1 offer.
Search firms resulted in 1 interview with 0 offers. Personal contacts resulted in 4 interviews with 1 offer.

E.C.'s entire campaign took 83 days and resulted in a position as director of engineering for a well-known company with a significant salary increase.

The letter he sent to me immediately after obtaining his job speaks for itself regarding how he felt about the campaign which he had just completed: "The battle is over. I have a new job. Substantial credit for the success belongs to you."

E.C.'s success story, however, didn't end then. Thirty days later the group vice president of his corporation flew out to talk to E.C. personally and to announce that he had been promoted to general manager of the division for which he had been hired initially as director of engineering.

From Assistant Project Manager to Director of Advertising

M.H. was the assistant project manager of a fund-raising program for a major university. Although she was very happy with her job, she was called in one day by her boss, the project director, and told that the program would terminate in five weeks.

M.H.'s background has been in advertising. In fact, the one other job she had held after graduating from college was in advertising for the garment industry. She had left this to become an assistant project manager at the university. However, the warning that her project was terminating left her with her MBA not yet completed.

M.H. thought herself qualified to be the director of advertising for a firm in the garment industry similar to the one she had already worked for. Her campaign involved a mailing to 200 firms in this industry, which resulted in five interviews and one offer. The offer was from the same firm that she had worked for earlier, but as director of advertising, two levels higher than the job she had previously held. Her new salary represented a 17% increase. Her campaign took approximately four weeks.

From Out of Work to Assistant Product Manager

F.R. was a reentry student of mine in a marketing class and out of work. Here is what F.R. wrote: "I received some news yesterday that's very exciting to me, and since I believe that your course and some of your ideas are greatly responsible for this good news, I wanted you to be one of the first to know. I was extended a job offer with a company, and in a position which is almost exactly what I was hoping for. The company is [a *Fortune* 500 company], and the position is assistant product manager. As I see it, your help was tremendously important, beyond the simple encouragement and interest you showed in my search: first, of course, were the direct mail techniques you taught in class, and more precisely your book which covered these techniques. Although I tailored your suggestions slightly toward my own needs, the guidelines were invaluable. These are the interviewing techniques that got me the job."

From Vice President of Operations
to Executive Vice President of Corporate Planning

M.A. was a vice president of operations of a major transportation company when he was suddenly terminated after a shake-up in higher management. During his 25-year career, he had never been out of work. *The Executive's Guide to Finding a Superior Job* was recommended to him by the dean of a major business school. By the time he began his campaign using the techniques in the book, he had already been out of work for approximately six months. As a consequence, he was then interviewing for all sorts of jobs, many far inferior to the one he had held previously.

Following my advice in the book, he stopped this practice, decided what he wanted to do, and ceased sending out a resume at all. He concentrated his campaign using the direct-mail-and-telephone technique contained in the TTP program in Chapter 7. Within ten weeks he had achieved a position as executive vice president of corporate planning in an international trading company, reporting to the president, with responsibilities for overseas agency coordination, corporate planning, expansion of administration, and other corporate matters. His salary was significantly higher than it had been before he was discharged from his former company.

From Engineer to Engineering Program Manager

R.E. was an engineer for a large company after having spent approximately seven years in the Air Force. However, his career was practically at a standstill because he had been an engineer at the basic level for over five years with no promotion. R.E. wanted increased responsibility and he wanted it fast. Although, of course, he would have liked to make more money, this was strictly incidental. Other criteria R.E. decided on for his superior job were that he wanted to be a program manager for an advanced engineering project, and he wanted to continue to work for a major company. Following the advice contained in the first edition of *The Executive's Guide to Finding a Superior Job,* he avoided personnel like the plague and sent letters to vice presidents of engineering in major companies, describing his specific accomplishments.

He was hired as a program manager for a major subcontractor, at a 20 percent salary increase, only three weeks after starting his campaign. In his note to me he said, "Thanks a million. Everything you said worked exactly as you said it would."

From MBA Student to Management Consultant

A.L. was a foreign student from Mexico who was completing his MBA studies in international business. He had held no previous job and was only 26 years old. His major ambition was to become a management consultant in a major consulting company. Failing this, he was interested in working on an interim basis as an export manager. His job campaign was complicated by the fact that many American firms did not wish to hire him because he was a noncitizen. He began a campaign three months before completing his MBA degree. He also emphasized the direct mail technique and sales letters described in Chapter 5. He constructed two entirely different sales letters, one for a management consultant job and the second for a position as an export manager. The management consultant list was small, fewer than 100 firms. The export manager campaign required approximately 500 letters sent to various companies exporting from California. These 500 sales letters yielded seven interviews and three job offers. However, none of these offers met with A.L.'s salary requirements or other aspects of what he felt to be a superior job.

A.L.'s 500 sales letters also brought another opportunity, which he was forced to consider at this point. Four firms contacted him by telephone and offered to hire him as an independent consultant for various operations in Mexico and South America that they were interested in. A.L. had to decide whether he wished to continue his campaign to be employed by someone else or actually go into independent consulting. He decided to continue his campaign.

The 100 sales letters sent out to major consulting firms resulted in only one face-to-face interview. However, he used the interviewing techniques discussed in Chapter 15, and this ultimately resulted in an offer at the highest salary received by anyone in A.L.'s MBA class.

Two years later, I received a call from A.L.'s wife. The call was to invite me to a surprise party. A.L. had been recruited by another major international consulting company to join an office in Mexico with a salary that would be the envy of many executives who have been in industry 20 years or more. A.L. had used my techniques again.

These job campaigns are only the tip of the iceberg. I have heard from many, many others who have successfully used *The Executive's Guide to Finding a Superior Job*. To express it in the words of one executive I unexpectedly ran into on vacation some time after he had read the book and put it into action, "Please tell everyone that these techniques really work."

23

Some Questions Frequently Asked About Getting a Superior Job

How can I tell the responsibility level of a new job before I am in it?

Many PEs will try to sell a job to candidates they want to hire, in some cases presenting a lower-level position as if it were in upper management. You can gauge the level of a job by whom it reports to, the salary, the title, additional privileges, and responsibilities.

None of these factors by itself is a certain indicator of job level. But taken together they present a pretty accurate picture. Be especially cautious of the PE's description of job responsibilities. Go over this point in detail with the PE and, if possible, get him to give you a written list of responsibilities.

Must I follow the exact form of the sample sales letters and responses to advertisements?

You need not use the exact formats for sales letters and other written communications, but you should follow the general concept. And keep one thing in mind about all the sample formats used in this book: they work. That doesn't mean you cannot be creative and develop variations on a theme. When I was in college I was taught a format for short position papers known as the "M-1 theme." The M-1 theme began with an introduction that stated the position the writer was taking. It was followed by three to five paragraphs, each presenting one fact in support of the writer's position. Each paragraph had three proofs of the main statement. The conclusion restated the introduction.

Now the M-1 theme wouldn't have earned anyone a literary award. But it was a clear way of stating a position. Students weren't required to use it for a graded paper; but if they did, and used it properly, they were just about guaranteed a passing grade. If they didn't—well, they took their chances. The formats described in this book are much the same; they are M-1 approaches to the problem. Use them properly and you are just about guaranteed a passing grade. Deviate very much and your results could go either way.

What is the best way to use high-level contacts during a job campaign?

High-level contacts are a good source of interviews (see Chapters 12 and 14). However, if you rely on such interviews too much you will be wasting time, since they tend to be of lower quality than interviews generated by sales letters, responses to advertisements, and other methods.

High-level contacts also make excellent references. As with all references, you should prepare your contacts first. Do not give a PE their names unless mutual interest is firmly established. Until that time, use the "title technique" to interest your PE.

How long should I remain with one company?

How long you remain with a company is entirely up to you. There is no general rule to follow, but there are certain factors you should consider. If you are making good career progress with one company and are happy, there is little reason to move. If the opposite is true, there are very real reasons to think about another job. But this is not a clear-cut case.

If you have been with a company only six months to a year you may want to move if the company has not fulfilled an important promise to you. It may be a promise for a promotion, for a different job, or for any other condition that is important to you. You might also move if an important part of your job hasn't worked out—for example, if there are serious personality conflicts between you and your boss or you and your co-workers. Finally, you may want to move if you are offered a position significantly higher than your current level. If you carry a title of vice president and are offered a position as president, you should certainly consider the opportunity.

In thinking about leaving your present job, you should consider how often you have changed jobs in the past. Suppose you remain only a year in your last two jobs and now, after six months to a year, you are offered a new position. I do not say you should not take the new position. But keep in mind that if it doesn't work out you may have difficulty explaining four jobs in less than as many years. After all, few PEs are interested in your service for a single year.

If you have spent some time with one company, the tenure you have built up will probably discourage you from leaving. If your retirement plan is funded solely by the company, you may lose all your interest in the plan if you leave. Just being on board with a company for a number of years increases your security, since the company would lose its investment in you if it decided to discharge you.

Then there is the unknown. There is no guarantee that a job in another company will be any better than your current job. Against the security of your present job you must weigh the advantages of a higher job level, greater responsibility, better compensation, better chances of promotion, or whatever benefits the new job offers.

I know that in a couple of years I'm going to have to leave my present company in order to reach my career goals. How can I prepare now for this eventual job campaign?

You should always be looking ahead in your career. Even if you are happy with your current job, you should prepare now for a future job campaign. One way to prepare yourself is through your performance on the job. Work hard to excel at your present position. You aren't going to have much of a career if you can't do something, and you aren't going to move up unless you can do it well.

You should also work hard to make yourself visible. Make sure that you are observed while performing and that the right people know about you and recognize your accomplishments. For example, if you just got a new job, ask to have a publicity release sent to trade magazines, your local newspaper, *The Wall Street Journal,* and other publications. It's good publicity for your company, but more important, it's good publicity for you. Headhunters use such releases as a source of candidates.

Another way to be visible is to write articles for professional magazines and journals, and present papers at professional conventions and symposiums. Become an active member of professional associations so that people from other companies get to know you and the type of work you can do.

If you are called by a headunter, either for a job or for recommendations, cultivate the contact and be as helpful as you can. If you are asked about your own background and are interested in the job, take the opportunity to advertise yourself and your accomplishments. In general, do everything you can to become an expert in your work, improve your performance, and let as many people as possible in your industry know.

I have heard that people get huge increases in salary—30 percent or more—for changing jobs. Is this true?

It is possible to negotiate a very large salary increase. However, this will usually happen only if a PE wants your services desperately and if you are currently employed at a senior level. If you are unemployed and not at a senior level, you can still do it, but you will have to become very skilled in job-hunting techniques. You must be willing to take high risks and to spend a lot of time on your job campaign. For the average executive job hunter, an unusually large salary increase is unlikely. The normal increase is 15 to 20 percent.

Should I try a new function in midcareer?

It is very difficult to change functions, especially if you are unemployed. Once you are hired, you will need to invest considerable time learning the new function before you reach parity with your old job level and compensation. On the other hand, changing functions may be worthwhile to get you out of a rut or allow you to attain a new level of achievement. In this case, you may need to take one step backward in order to take three steps forward.

Whether you want to accept the risks of a midcareer change for a career in a new business function is a decision that you must make yourself. To minimize the risks, you should find out as much as you can about your aptitude in the new area. Take interest tests at a local college or a psychological testing service. Next, talk to your present employer about your desires. You may be able to transfer departments in your present company. In this case, you need only adjust to a new function, rather than to both a new function and a new company.

Do you have any special tips for women executives seeking jobs in traditionally male fields?

Not too long ago, I was approached by a young woman who had been a buyer in a major aerospace firm for several years. She had recently obtained an MBA in marketing and wanted to be a marketing manager.

Her own company discouraged her, however, and would not permit her to transfer to marketing. She wanted to know whether I thought she could become a marketing manager in a major aerospace company, a function clearly male-dominated.

My answer was that she could, but that it was going to be tough and that she should be prepared for some hard knocks and a longer-than-usual campaign. The key was to use the techniques I recommend for everyone: She must prove that she was clearly superior by documenting past accomplishments in the same or a similar job. And, more than ever, she must thoroughly understand the market, the customer, and the product before she interviewed. I sent her on her way thinking that if she was willing to relocate geographically she could probably get the job she wanted in three or four months.

But I was wrong. She applied the techniques and got the job she wanted after only a six-week campaign. Nor did she need to relocate. Although this type of job in this particular industry is still usually held by a man, any manager has to be primarily interested in the bottom line of his (or her) organization. If you can convince the PE that your presence will improve the organization's performance, you'll get the job.

I am 57 and was recently laid off. Is there any hope that I can get a job?

Executive job hunters have improved their job situations even when they have been forced to retire at age 70. However, it would be misleading to say that age is not a factor in job hunting. It is. But many other factors—experience, background, and accomplishments—are far more important than age. In your job campaign you should accentuate positive factors to such a degree—stressing how your experience and accomplishments are suited to a specific job—that they far outweigh any negative factors. To sum up, there is more than hope. You can get a superior job!

I look young for my age and my level of management. Should I try to look older during a job campaign?

If you feel youth is going to be a problem, there is no reason not to use cosmetic tricks to make yourself look older so you can get a superior job. There are many ways to do this. Wear glasses. Grow a mustache. Concentrate on presenting a dignified appearance, dressing conservatively, and speaking slowly and with confidence.

If you feel you look too old, you can use various techniques to appear younger. Dye your hair. Wear contact lenses. Wear a hairpiece. All such changes are perfectly acceptable when you are on a job campaign.

Remember, job hunting is a competitive situation. Vanity has nothing to do with it. If something can help you beat the competition, do it.

I've been out of work for some time and have done a few of the things you suggest. How should I proceed?

Part of the trick in finding a superior job is organizing your campaign carefully and integrating the various phases. If you are unemployed and have been looking for a while, forget what you've done before. Adopt a positive attitude, lay your plans according to this book, and have at it.

I am confined to a wheelchair. I seem to be able to get interviews, but the shock of seeing me in a wheelchair seems to kill my chances of getting a job offer. How should I handle this?

If you have a conspicuous handicap, you should hint about it in a preinterview contact with the PE so he will not be shocked when he sees you. Naturally, a physical handicap has nothing to do with your job performance and your ability to make money for your company. These are the primary considerations to any PE.

Now let's talk about what form your preinterview hint might take. In a sales letter you could turn your handicap into an advantage by using an opening/attention getter that mentioned your disability: "Being in a wheelchair didn't prevent me from making over $1 million for my company last year."

After the interview has been set up by phone, if you've got the right personality for this type of remark, use it: "I'm going to show up in a wheelchair, so I'll need a little help if you're on the second floor. But don't let that turn you off; I'm one hell of an engineer."

The object is to alert the PE so that when he sees you for the first time, he will be focusing his attention on your accomplishments and what you can do for his company.

Many executives have written to me about less conspicuous handicaps, such as having been in prison. The key here is not to lie, but not to volunteer information until you've made a sale. If your PE thinks you are going to make money for him, you are going to get hired, regardless of your background.

What is the primary factor in getting a superior job?

The primary factor in getting a superior job is the ability to convince PEs that you can do a superior job for them.

24

It's Up to You

Being an Expert Isn't Everything

At this point, you have read enough material to be an expert in job hunting and to get a superior job. You understand the importance of a positive mental attitude. You know how to define your professional career objective before you start. You understand the importance of planning your job campaign, and you know how to do so. You are familiar with the techniques necessary for developing a superior resume, and you know how to generate high-quality interviews through sales letters, advertisements, the telephone, headhunters, and friends.

If you are employed, you have mastered the techniques of job hunting in secret. If you have just left the service, you know how to overcome the special job-hunting problems faced by former military executives. If you are unemployed, you are not dismayed, because you know you have real advantages over your employed competitors in job hunting. Further, with your command of techniques for interviewing and negotiating you look forward to job hunting as a challenge; you enjoy trying to get a superior job offer from each interview.

Knowing all these things, you still realize that everything is up to you. All this knowledge and all these techniques are worthless unless you put them to use. If after you have read this book thoroughly you do not act, all the effort on both our parts has been wasted.

If you aren't looking for a job at the present time, put the book away. The knowledge you have gained will give you a new self-confidence and freedom of action in your present job. When the time comes to start your campaign, take out the book and read it again. Regardless of your circumstances, the techniques described will give you the confidence and ability to find a superior job.

Index

advertisements, 18, 58–73
  advantages of, 58
  blind, 61–62, 101–102
  drafting responses to, 63–64, 187–188
  response frequency and, 63
  salary information in, 64, 65
  sales letters compared to, 72–73
  sample responses to, 65–72
  telephone responses to, 65, 67
  two-letter responses to, 125–126
  see also self-advertisement
age, 44, 191–192
American Management Associations (AMA)
  Executive Compensation Service of, 153–154
  seminars of, 90
answering services, 102
attitude, 3–8
  importance of, in job hunting, 3–4, 7–8
  during interviews, 3, 5–6
  knowledge of personal strengths and, 6, 8
  resume and development of positive, 5
  setbacks and, 4–5, 8

Better Business Bureau, 94, 181
blind ads, 61–62, 101–102
body language, 139

colleges/universities
  accreditation of, 44–45

psychological tests available from, 148–149
  as sources of compensation information, 153
  see also education
company as job objective, 12
compensation
  in advertisement responses, 64–65
  as criterion for headhunters, 93, 94
  headhunter knowledge of, 95
  information sources on, 152–154, 164–165, 171
  as job objective, 14
  see also salary
concentration strategy, 113–118
  development of, 113–115
  disadvantages of, 117–118
  successful use of, 116–117
  third-party approach in, 115–116
Consultants and Consulting Organizations Directory, 52
costs of job campaign, 26
counselors, *see* job counselors
courtesy interviews, 109–111
credibility
  in sales letters, 43–45, 57
  in self-advertisement, 84

debriefings after interviews, 163–164
directories
  of associations, 87
  of prospective employers, 50–51, 75
  of publicity release outlets, 89
  of publishers, 85–86
  of search firms, 52

Directory of Executive Recruiters, 52
Directory of Publishing Opportunities in Business, Administration, and Economics, 86
Directory of Publishing Opportunities in Journals and Periodicals, 86
Drucker, Peter, on job-loss fear, 1

education
    accreditation of schools and, 44–45
    in responses to advertisements, 64
    in self-advertisement, 84
    see also colleges/universities
employers
    handling questions about former, 138–139
    see also prospective employers
employment agencies, vi, 19
    candidate characteristics and, 93–94
    interviews with, 19, 95–96
    references supplied to, 94–95
    resume distribution by, 96–97
    salary history and, 95
    search firms compared to, 91–93
    as source of compensation information, 153
    techniques for dealing with, 94
employment applications, 54–55, 162
Encyclopedia of Associations, 87
ethics
    in gathering information, 120–121
    in job campaign, 127
Executive Employment Guide, 52

Firms Doing Executive Search, 52
follow-up letters, 21, 143–145
friends, 108–112
    advantages of relying on, 108
    contacts of, in letter-and-telephone campaign, 126–127
    courtesy interviews and, 109–111
    disadvantages of relying on, 108–109
    as source of compensation information, 153
    two-groups-of-names method for using, 109–110
fringe benefits, 170–171, 174
function as job objective, 13

Garfield, Charles A., on mental rehearsal, 134–135

Guide to American Directories for Compiling Mailing Lists, 50

handicaps, 192
headhunters, *see* employment agencies; search firms

industry as job objective, 11–12
information
    directories as source of, 50–52, 75, 85–87, 89
    gathering of, for interviews, 119–121, 129–132
    from personnel managers, 59–61, 162–165
    sources of compensation, 152–154, 164–165, 171
    unusual sources of, 119–121
interviews, 128–145
    arrival time for, 135
    attitude and, 3, 5–6
    basic principles of, 128–129
    body language in, 139
    closing of, with a sale, 142–143
    contacts plus letter-and-telephone campaign for obtaining, 126–127
    courtesy, 109–111
    debriefings after, 163–164
    developing questions for, 130–132
    expert interviewers in, 140
    first impressions in, 135
    first names and, 135–136
    gaining control of, 136–137
    gauging progress in, 141
    with headhunters, 19, 95–96
    honing technique in, 111–112
    information gathering for, 119–121, 129–132
    mental rehearsal for, 4, 134–135
    number of, from sales letter campaign, 53–54, 72–73
    with personnel managers, 162–165
    preparing for, 20–21, 130–132
    procedures for setting up, 20, 129–130
    questions about employers during, 138–139
    requests for, from sales letters, 55–56
    salary discussion in, 137–138
    smoking during, 136
    solicitation of, by search firms, 97–98

interviews *(continued)*
   stress, 132–134
   telephone, 55–56, 60–61, 74
   telephone techniques for obtaining,
      74–81
   writing follow-up letters for, 21, 143–
      145

job counselors, 177–181
   advantages of using, 178–180
   disadvantages of using, 177–178
   selection of, 180–181
job creation, 124–125
job offers
   acceptance of, 21
   salary negotiation and, 170–176

knockout factors, 36

letters
   interview follow-up, 21, 143–145
   see also sales letters
level as job objective, 13–14, 187
location as job objective, 14–15

mailgrams for blind ad responses, 61–
   62
mailing lists, 18, 50–52
mental visualization (rehearsal), 4, 134–
   135
military service, 151–160
   compensation information and, 152–
      154
   job-hunting problems after leaving,
      151–152
   revealing rank in, 159–160
   stating accomplishments of, in busi-
      ness terms, 154–159
Million Dollar Directory (Dun & Brad-
      street), 51

negotiating, 21, 170–176, 190
   counteroffers in, 173–175
   handling job offers in, 175–176
   indirect approach in, 172–173
   personnel manager's role in, 164–
      165
   and prenegotiation stage, 170–171
   and present salary, 171–172
   several offers simultaneously, 175–
      176

objectives
   defining job, 9–15
   for sales letters, 37–38

PEs, *see* prospective employers
personnel department
   employment applications from, 54–
      55, 162
   methods for avoiding, 53
   rejection notices from, 54–55
personnel managers, 161–165
   avoiding contact with, 161
   debriefings and, 163–164
   obtaining information from, 59–61,
      154, 164–165
   role of, in salary negotiations, 164–
      165
   screening interviews with, 165
   as source of compensation informa-
      tion, 154, 164–165
planning
   for costs of job campaign, 26
   framework for, 16–17
   for the interview, 20–21
   for length of job campaign, 22
   postinterview phase in, 21
   preinterview phase in, 17–20
postinterview letters, 21, 143–145
*Principal Business Directories for Build-
      ing Mailing Lists,* 50
printing of sales letters, 17, 19, 52–53
professional associations
   directory of, 87
   membership in, as self-advertise-
      ment, 87–88
   presenting papers before, 90
   as source of compensation informa-
      tion, 154
   speaking before, 86–87
prospective employers (PEs)
   directories of, 50–51, 75
   discussing job advertisements with,
      60–61
   research on, 5, 6, 50–51, 75
psychological tests, 146–150
   disadvantages of, 146–148
   obtaining samples of, 148–149
   rules for "passing," 150
publicity releases for self-advertisement,
      88–89, 189
publishers, directories of, 85–86

recordkeeping for sales campaigns, 19, 57
reference checks, 92, 166–169
  bad references in, 167–168
  superior references in, 168–169
references, 13, 14
  on employment applications, 55
  high-level contacts as, 188
  preparation of, for reference checks, 168–169
  protection of, 169
  in secret job campaign, 102–103
  supplying of, to headhunters, 94–95
Register of Corporations, Directors, and Executives (Standard & Poor's), 51
rejection notices, 54–55
research
  preinterview, 130–132
  on prospective employers, 5, 6, 50–51, 75
resume(s), 33–34
  avoiding widespread distribution of, 96–97
  developing a positive attitude by re-reading, 5
  handling requests for, 78, 81
  mention of, in sales letter, 46
  salary in, vi
resume preparation, 17, 27–34
  form for, 28–32
  by professionals, 27–28, 179
  special and short assignments in, 33
  of special resumes, 21
Rodman, Dr. Irwin, on psychological testing, 147

salary
  in advertisement responses, 64–65
  discussion of, in interviews, 137–138
  headhunter knowledge of, 95
  information sources on, 152–154, 164–165, 171
  as job objective, 14
  negotiation for, 21, 170–176, 190
  preinterview discussion of, 56, 80
  statement of, in resume, vi
sales letters, 35–57, 182–188
  advantages of, 35–37, 72–73
  call to action in, 45
  credibility in, 43–45, 57

explanations in, 41–42, 57
  interview requests and, 55–56
  in letter-and-telephone campaigns, 124–125
  mailing lists for, 18, 50–52
  mailing of, 18–20, 51–52, 121–124
  after military service, 155–159
  motivation section in, 42–43, 57
  objectives for, 37–38
  opening/attention getters in, 39–41, 57
  printing of, 17, 19, 52–53
  reasons for success of, 37
  recordkeeping for, 19, 57
  responses from, 53–55, 72–73
  to search firms, 47–49, 101
  second, 19–20, 55–57
  secrecy and, 99–101
  in self-advertisements, 83–84
  in telephone campaigns, 77–79, 126–127
  telephone number in, 46–47, 55
  third-party, 100–101
  writing of, 17, 19, 37–49
search firms
  candidate characteristics and, 93–94
  compiling lists of, 52
  employment agencies compared to, 91–93
  interviews with, 19, 95–96
  references supplied to, 93–95
  salary history and, 95
  sales letters to, 47–49, 101
  as source of compensation information, 153
  telephone solicitations from, 97–98
secrecy, 99–104
  blind ads and, 61–62, 101–102
  friends and, 109
  job campaign length and, 103–104
  in self-advertisement, 84
  third-party telephone campaign and, 102–103
secretaries
  avoiding, on telephone, 76–77
self-advertisement, 82–90, 189–190
  article-writing for, 85–86
  disadvantages of, 82
  methods for successful, 82–84
  organization membership for, 87–88
  presenting papers as, 90

self-advertisement *(continued)*
  publicity releases for, 88–89, 189
  secrecy in, 84
  seminars as, 89–90
  speech-making for, 86–87
seminars as self-advertisement, 89–90
smoking, 136
specialization, job creation and, 124–
  125
speeches for self-advertisement, 86–87
Standard Directory of Advertisers, 51
Standard Rate and Data Services
  (SRDS), 89
stationery
  for advertisement responses, 64
  for sales letters, 53
stress interviews, 132–134

telephone
  answering services for, 102
  dealing with secretaries on, 76–77
  interviews on, 55–56, 60–61, 74
  search firm solicitation by, 97–98
telephone number
  in blind ad responses, 62, 101
  in sales letters, 46–47, 55
  in self-advertisements, 84
Telephone Training Program (TTP),
  18–19, 74–81
  described, 74–75

limitations of, 79–80
obtaining key names through, 75
reaching hiring executives through,
  76–77
for responding to advertisements, 65,
  67
speaking with hiring executives in,
  77–81
third-party approach in, 102–103
tests, *see* psychological tests
TTP, *see* Telephone Training Program
*Thomas Register of American Manufac-
  turers,* 51
travel, expenses for, 26

unemployment, 105–107
  age and, 191
  determination and sense of urgency
    in, 107, 175
  freedom of action and, 106
  headhunters and, 93–94
  lack of conflict of interest and, 106–
    107
  sales letters and, 46
  time advantage and, 105–106

women in male-dominated fields, 190–
  191
Writer's Market, 85
writing as self-advertisement, 85–86